PRAISE FOR SHANNON KAISER

"One of the freshest voices in mental health and wellness, Shannon is on a mission to empower others to be true to themselves and live their full potential."

—**Marci Shimoff,** *New York Times* bestselling author of *Happy for No Reason and Chicken Soup for the Woman's Soul*

"Shannon is an absolute goddess. She's a beautiful example of what is possible when you free yourself from self-criticism, blame, and guilt and choose love instead. I am in total adoration of this woman and that's because of how in love she is with herself, the world, and life! Thank you, Shannon, for being such a light. Readers, you are in for a treat!"

—**Mel Wells,** eating psychology coach and bestselling author of *The Goddess Revolution*

"Shannon's blazing one hell of a self-love trial for others to show up, release fear, and live life fully. You know, one where your dreams come true and we live happily ever after in love, with ourselves! The world needs this self-love injection, and so do you."

—**Emma Mildon,** bestselling author of *The Soul Searcher's Handbook and Evolution of Goddess*

"Shannon offers easy-to-absorb advice to help you become your happiest, most loved, highest-potential self—and best of all, she makes it a fun process. My kind of gal."

—**Karen Salmansohn,** bestselling author of *How to Be Happy, Dammit*

"Shannon Kaiser is an incredible woman on a mission to help people find peace, happiness, and fulfillment in their lives. Her desire to serve others shines through all of her work."

—**Gabrielle Bernstein,** *New York Times* bestselling author of *May Cause Miracles*

"Shannon Kaiser inspires people to ditch what doesn't serve them and follow their paths to true joy and satisfaction."

—**mindbodygreen**

ALSO BY SHANNON KAISER

BOOKS

*The Self-Love Experiment: Fifteen Principles for Becoming
More Kind, Compassionate, and Accepting of Yourself*

*Adventures for Your Soul: 21 Ways to Transform Your Habits
and Reach Your Full Potential*

*Find Your Happy: An Inspirational Guide to
Loving Life to Its Fullest*

ONLINE COURSES

How to Find Your Calling & Live a Life with More Meaning
(mindbodygreen Video Course)

Make Happiness a Way of Life (Daily Om Course)

Embrace Your Single Self (Daily Om Course)

Find Your Happy

Daily Mantras

365 DAYS OF MOTIVATION FOR A HAPPY, PEACEFUL, AND FULFILLING LIFE

SHANNON KAISER

BEYOND WORDS
Hillsboro, Oregon

To Steve Harris

Thank you for your endless support and helping me
make my dreams come true—you helped me get
this work out into the world.

BEYOND WORDS

20827 N.W. Cornell Road, Suite 500
Hillsboro, Oregon 97124-9808
503-531-8700 / 503-531-8773 fax
www.beyondword.com

First Beyond Words paperback edition February 2018
Copyright © 2018 by Shannon Kaiser
Originally published by Balboa Press, 2014

For information about special discounts for bulk purchases, please contact Beyond Words
Special Sales at 503-531-8700 or specialsales@beyondword.com.

Managing Editor: Lindsay S. Easterbrooks-Brown
Editor: Emily Einolander
Proofreader: Kristin Thiel
Design: Sara E. Blum

Manufactured in the United States of America
10 9 8 7 6 5 4 3 2 1

Library of Congress Control Number: 2017960900

The corporate mission of Beyond Words Publishing, Inc.: *Inspire to Integrity*

Contents

Free Audio Download: "I Am Peace" Meditation xvi

Introduction xvii

Day 1: I Am Abundant and Secure. 1

Day 2: I Am Brave and Courageous with My Heart. 2

Day 3: I Release All Worry. I Celebrate What Could Go Right. 4

Day 4: All My Needs Are Always Met. 5

Day 5: All I Desire Is on Its Way to Me. 6

Day 6: I Am Open and Willing to Live My Life in New Ways. 7

Day 7: I Turn My Reaction into Compassion. 8

Day 8: Everything Is in Divine Order. 9

Day 9: I Am Surrounded by Love. I Am Protected. 10

Day 10: I Get What I Focus On. 11

Day 11: The Fastest Way to Fulfillment Is to Live My Values. 12

Day 12: I Feel with My Heart. 13

Day 13: I Am Open to the Things I Do Not Know Yet. 14

Day 14: Abundance and Joy Are My Birthright. 15

Day 15: I See the Light and Love in Others. 16

Day 16: When I Follow My Passions, My Purpose Is Revealed. 17

Day 17: When I Clean Up My Thoughts, I Clean Up My Life. 18

Day 18: Everything I Need Is Inside of Me. 19

Day 19: I Believe in the Good of Mankind. 20

Day 20: What I Seek Is on Its Way to Me. 21

Day 21: I Recognize and Honor the Light Inside of Me. 22

Day 22: The Right Choice Is the Choice That Feels Expansive
and Joyful. 23

Day 23: I Am Not Alone. 24

Day 24: My Stress Is Trying to Tell Me Something. 25

Day 25: Regardless of the Outcome, I Am Taken Care Of. 26

Day 26: I Celebrate Life's Little Victories. 27

Day 27: Needing Someone Is Not a Weakness. It Is an Act of Self-Love. 28

Day 28: I Am Only Isolated by My Illusion. I Perceive Others
with Love. 29

Day 29: The Present Moment Is All That Matters. 30

Day 30: Clutter Is a Byproduct of Indecision. I Remove All Extra
Stuff from My Life. 31

Day 31: The First Step to Improving the World Is to Improve Myself. 33

Day 32: I Release My Need to Get There. 34

Day 33: Instead of Focusing on the Anger, I Focus on Healing the Pain. 35

Day 34: I Respect Expiration Dates. 36

Day 35: My Life Is a Courageous, Creative Adventure. 37

Day 36: Every Next Level of My Life Will Demand a
Different Version of Me. 38

Day 37: Everything Happens at the Right Time and Place. 39

Day 38: The More I Know Myself, the More I Can Be Myself. 40

Day 39: Forgiveness Isn't about Freeing Me from My Past.
It Is about Opening Up My Future. 41

Day 40: It's Not about Where I Am Going but Who I Become. 42

Day 41: I Don't Take Myself Too Seriously. I See the
Lightheartedness in This Moment. 43

Day 42: Everything's Going to Be All Right. It Always Works
Out in the End. 44

Day 43: Life Is about Detours. I Take the Road Less Traveled
and Embrace the Unknown. 45

Day 44: My Dreams Are the Signature to My Potential. 46

Day 45: I Trust My Intuition. 47

Day 46: I Am Not Damaged or Wounded. There Is Nothing
Wrong with Me. 48

Day 47: Anything I Give My Attention to Will Flourish and Grow. 49

Day 48: Self-Love Is Not about How I Look or What I Do—It's about
How I Live. 50

Day 49: I Think from My Heart. 51

Day 50: It Is Okay to Change My Mind. 52

Day 51: Embrace the Space between Where I Am and
Where I Want to Be. 53

Day 52: My Beliefs Do Not Define Me. I Am Willing to See Other
Perspectives without Judgment. 54

Day 53: My Inner Child Wants to Play. 55

Day 54: This Is the Life I Want to Live. 56

Day 55: I Listen to the Guidance Coming My Way. 57

Day 56: I Witness Situations without Judgment. 58

Day 57: I Am Hurting, and That Is Okay. 59

Day 58: I Am Where I Am—Not Where I Think I Should Be. 60

Day 59: I Wait for the Right Time. 61

Day 60: I Surrender All Expectations. 62

Day 61: I Open Myself Up to Transformational Love. 64

Day 62: I Have Unique Gifts and Talents That the World Needs. ... 65

Day 63: Gratitude Is the Life Force of Everything. 66

Day 64: I Have the Courage to Be Imperfect. 67

Day 65: The Worst Is Behind Me. 68

Day 66: I Gracefully Accept All Changes Happening in My Life. ... 69

Day 67: I Am Vibrant and in Picture-Perfect Health. 70

Day 68: It Isn't What I Have That Matters. It Is What I Do
with What I Have. 71

Day 69: My Dreams Will Only Succeed When I Take a
Chance on Them. 72

Day 70: It's This or Something Better. 73

Day 71: I Believe in What I Can't See. 74

Day 72: Fear of the Unknown Is a Byproduct of Settling. I Don't Settle. 75

Day 73: My Soul Is Rooting for Me. 76

Day 74: I Feel My Fear and Do It Anyway. 77

Day 75: My Loneliness Is Not an Invitation to Settle. 78

Day 76: I Am Kind to Myself. I Know I Am Doing the Best I Can. ... 79

Day 77: Daily Action Cultivates Confidence and Clarity. 80

Day 78: I Can Try Again. 81

Day 79: I Don't Need a Reason to Help Others. 82

Day 80: I Love My Body because of What It Has Overcome. 83

Day 81: I Am Compassionate with Myself. It Takes Time to Heal. ... 84

Day 82: I Stop Blowing Myself Off. 85

Day 83: I Do Not Cheat on My Future with My Past. 86

Day 84: My Uniqueness Is What Makes Me Outstanding. 87

Day 85: Thinking I Don't Have a Choice Is a Choice. 88

Day 86: I Am Accountable for My Own Life. 89

Day 87: I Don't Romanticize the Past. I Choose to Be Present. ... 90

Day 88: I Am Not What People Say I Am. 91

Day 89: I Learn the Way on the Way. 92

Day 90: I Let Go of What the Universe Is Asking Me to Release. ... 93

Day 91: My Purpose Is to Live More on Purpose. 95

Day 92: Pleasure Is My Priority. 96

Day 93: My Plan B Could Be Better than Plan A. 97

Day 94: I Am Enchanted with Life. I See the Beauty in Everything. 98

Day 95: Part of Loving Myself Is Letting Others Help Me. 99

Day 96: Where I Live Feels Like a Home. 100

Day 97: How I Feel Is More Important than How I Look. 101

Day 98: My Emotional Pain Shows Me What Needs to Change. 102

Day 99: No One Can Make Me Feel "Less than" without

My Permission. 103

Day 100: I Appreciate the Person I See in the Mirror. 104

Day 101: I Surrender the Struggle. 105

Day 102: I Am Making a Bigger Impact than I Realize. 106

Day 103: I Have Determination and Willpower. 107

Day 104: I Have a Support System That Would Do Anything for Me. 108

Day 105: I Don't Waste Time with Negative Thoughts. 109

Day 106: I Embrace My Emotions. 110

Day 107: I Celebrate Others' Successes. 111

Day 108: I Nurture My Instincts. 112

Day 109: I Imagine Myself Living My Ideal Life. 113

Day 110: My Creative Pursuits Are Rewarded. 114

Day 111: It Is Not Flowing because It Is Not the Right Time. 115

Day 112: I Am Unapologetic about What Makes Me Happy. 116

Day 113: Self-Love Is a Practice I Show Up for Daily. 117

Day 114: I Celebrate the Mini Miracles. 118

Day 115: I Am Comfortable in the Silence. 119

Day 116: I Retreat Inward for Inspiration. 120

Day 117: When I Give, I Also Receive. 121

Day 118: Everything Has an Expiration Date. 122

Day 119: What I See in Life Depends Greatly on What

I'm Looking For. 123

Day 120: My Life Is in Perfect Balance When I Listen to My Heart. 124

Day 121: Things Fall Apart because Better Things Are

Falling into Place. 125

Day 122: I Let Go So I Can Let Myself Grow. 126

Day 123: There Is Nothing to Fear. Love Is Here. 128

Day 124: I Go Before I Know. 129

Day 125: New Opportunities for Happiness Are on

Their Way to Me. 130

Day 126: I Break Free from All That Is Holding Me Back. 131

Day 127: I Commit to My Desired Outcome. 132

Day 128: The Fastest Way to Improve My Self-Confidence
Is to Do the Thing I Fear. 133

Day 129: I Pray for the Highest Good of All Involved. 134

Day 130: I Am Only Trapped by My Illusion. 135

Day 131: I Find a Way to Keep Going. 136

Day 132: Who I Become in the Process of Reaching My Goals Is
More Important than Achieving Them. 137

Day 133: It Is Refreshing to Give Life to Old Projects. 138

Day 134: It Isn't Who I Am That Holds Me Back. It's
Who I Think I Am Not. 139

Day 135: Things Move Fast When They Are Right. 140

Day 136: Communication Can Save Any Situation. 141

Day 137: I Have Loving Allowance for Others to Be Who They
Are Instead of Who I Think They Need to Be. 142

Day 138: I Love Me. 143

Day 139: I Know When to Move On. 144

Day 140: There Are Infinite Resources Available to Me. 145

Day 141: My Anxiety Is Not Based on Reality. 146

Day 142: I Am Tenacious with My Goals. They Are Actualized
with Love. 147

Day 143: I Can Only Take Responsibility for Me. 148

Day 144: I Am Well. 149

Day 145: I Am Calm in the Chaos. 150

Day 146: I Replace Judgment with Curiosity. 151

Day 147: I Am Only Trapped by My Own Illusions. 152

Day 148: I Know It Is Not about Me. 153

Day 149: I Passed the Test. 154

Day 150: I Detach from the Drama Around Me. 155

Day 151: I Explore All My Options. 156

Day 152: I've Done Nothing Wrong. 157

Day 153: My Heart Never Lies. 159

Day 154: The Fastest Way to Solve the Problem Is to Stop
Participating in the Problem. 160

Day 155: I Don't Second-Guess Myself. 161

Day 156: I Take Time to Rest. 162

Day 157: I Am Flooded with Gratitude. 163

Day 158: I Turn My Anxiety into Excitement. 164

Day 159: I See Love Everywhere. 165

Day 160: The Best Advice Is Felt in My Heart, Not Directed
from My Head. 166

Day 161: Everything Happens for a Reason. 167

Day 162: I Seek Out Sanctuary. 168

Day 163: Things Aren't Always What They Seem. 169

Day 164: I Attract What I Want by Being What I Desire. 170

Day 165: Life Is a Balancing Act of Holding On and Letting Go. 171

Day 166: Change Is the Catalyst to Harmony. 172

Day 167: I Put Down the Pity Party. 173

Day 168: I Am the Hero of My Own Life Story. 174

Day 169: I Am Unapologetic about My Needs and Desires. 175

Day 170: When Two or More People Are Gathered, Miracles Happen. . . . 176

Day 171: I Love My Life. 177

Day 172: I'm Not Influenced by What Was. 178

Day 173: When I Am Feeling Angst, I Ask, "What Is This Situation
Trying to Teach Me?" 179

Day 174: My Positive Thoughts Create Desired Results. 180

Day 175: I Acknowledge My Discomforts. 181

Day 176: I Refuse to Participate in the Drama of the World. 182

Day 177: Time Is on My Side. 183

Day 178: I Don't Have to Move On to Let Go. 184

Day 179: It's Okay to Change My Mind. 185

Day 180: I Don't Take Anything Personally—It's Not
about Me. 186

Day 181: I Am the Kindest Person I Know. 187

Day 182: I See the World as a Beautiful, Kind, and Loving Place. 188

Day 183: I Can Find Comfort in My Pain. 189

Day 184: I Was Born to Do This. It's Go Time. 190

Day 185: Real Love Is Unconditional and Never Ends. 192

Day 186: When I Cherish Myself, I Spend My Time Wisely. 193

Day 187: I Am More on Track than I Give Myself Credit For. 194

Day 188: I Have the Courage to Become Who I Am Meant to Be. 195

Day 189: Just Because It Hasn't Been Done Doesn't
Mean It Can't Be. 196

Day 190: It's All for Me. 197

Day 191: I Take Responsibility for My Happiness. 198

Day 192: The Grass Is Greenest Where I Stand. 199

Day 193: I Don't Wait in Vain. 200

Day 194: I Don't Keep Score. 201

Day 195: Money Will Always Flow. My Source of Abundance
Is Divine. 202

Day 196: I Am Extraordinary. 203

Day 197: It Is Time to Say Good-Bye to the Life I Know—I Let
Myself Grow. 204

Day 198: Not Everything in My Life Deserves My Attention. 205

Day 199: What I'm Searching for Is Not Out There—It Is in Me. 206

Day 200: I Evolve According to My Own Reaction to
Each Situation. 207

Day 201: I Take a Leap of Faith. 208

Day 202: My Life Gets Better When I Push through My
Comfort Zone. 209

Day 203: All My Fears Are Fantasy. 210

Day 204: I Am Who I Needed When I Was Younger. 211

Day 205: Following My Heart Is the Most Responsible Thing I
Can Do for My Well-Being. 212

Day 206: Even the Darkness Has Its Wonders. 213

Day 207: There Is Only One Me. 214

Day 208: The More Me I Show, the More My Life Will Flow. 215

Day 209: When I Heal Myself, I Help to Heal the World. 216

Day 210: I Can Reinvent Myself at Any Time. 217

Day 211: When I Nurture the Inside, the Outside Will Flourish. 219

Day 212: I Do One Thing Every Day for Which My Future Self
Will Hug Me. 220

Day 213: I Create My Own Extraordinary Reality. 221

Day 214: I Am Confident in Beliefs That Work for Me. 222

Day 215: I Commit to Staying Open-Minded. 223

Day 216: No One Else Knows What's Best for Me. 224

Day 217: What I See in Others Is a Reflection of Myself. 225

Day 218: When I Look at the World as a Good, Happy,
and Kind Place, Good, Happy, and Kind Things Come to Me. 226

Day 219: I Am Worth It, and I Have a Lot to Give. 227

Day 220: I Don't Waste Time with Negative Thoughts. 228

Day 221: My Life Gets Better by Change, Not Chance. 229

Day 222: Kindness Wins. 230

Day 223: When I Speak My Truth, It Gives Others Permission
to Do the Same. 231

Day 224: I Disengage from All Harmful Activities. 232

Day 225: I Am Ready to Change and Embrace New Patterns
and Ways of Being. 233

Day 226: Every Situation Is an Opportunity to Choose Love
Over Fear. 234

Day 227: All Is in the Right Order. 235

Day 228: Passion Is My Purpose—It Leads Me Forward. 236

Day 229: Love Is the Key to My Success. 237

Day 230: I Pause in My Pleasure. 238

Day 231: Regrets Are Opportunities to Learn and Grow. 239

Day 232: You Know the Truth by the Way You Feel. 240

Day 233: I Don't Use Avoidance Tactics. 241

Day 234: I Am Patient with Myself. 242

Day 235: I Give Up Control. 243

Day 236: I Stay on Projects Until I See a Successful Conclusion. 244

Day 237: I Give Others the Benefit of the Doubt. 245

Day 238: The Little Things I Do Make a Big Difference. 246

Day 239: My Self-Respect and Dignity Are My Top Priority. 247

Day 240: I Can Laugh at Myself. 248

Day 241: I Eat My Food Guilt-Free. 249

Day 242: I Am Generous with My Time and Energy.
I Support Those I Love. 250

Day 243: My Self-Sabotaging Habits Have a Message for Me.
I Listen to the Guidance. 251

Day 244: I Am Not Powerless. 252

Day 245: I Start Each Day with a Grateful Heart. 254

Day 246: I Stop Worrying How It Will Happen and Start
Trusting That It Will Happen. 255

Day 247: I Am Responsible for Changing My Behavior Until I
Get What I Want. 256

Day 248: I Stop Worrying about Debt. 257

Day 249: I Forgive Ex-Lovers. 258

Day 250: When I Help Others, I Help Myself. 259

Day 251: It Is Okay Not to Be Okay. 260

Day 252: What I Want Wants Me Too. 261

Day 253: I Show the World My Weird, Crazy, Beautiful Self. 262

Day 254: I Inspire Others with My Own Bigness. 263

Day 255: I Live My Values. 264

Day 256: I Stay Hopeful and Optimistic in Difficult Situations. 265

Day 257: I See Everyone as an Equal. 266

Day 258: I Accept That Good Is Good Enough. 267

Day 259: I Am Comfortable Saying Thank You. 268

Day 260: I Set High Expectations. 269

Day 261: I Am Resilient. 270

Day 262: Setbacks Do Not Define Me. They Nudge Me into
a New Awareness. 271

Day 263: I Reward Myself with Simple Luxuries. 272

Day 264: I Leave All Unhealthy Situations. 273

Day 265: My Inner Voice Is Trustworthy. 274

Day 266: It Is Already Done. 275

Day 267: I Detach from All Troubling Situations and Surround
Them with Love. 276

Day 268: I Go for What I Want, Not Just What I Think
Is Possible. 277

Day 269: Opportunities Fly at Me. 278

Day 270: I Am a "Why Not" Person. 279

Day 271: I Am Always on the Edge of My Potential. 281

Day 272: My Life Is an Experiment. I Embrace the Exploration. 282

Day 273: I Smile at Strangers. 283

Day 274: All New Things Require Discomfort. 284

Day 275: I Set Fun and Recreation Goals. 285

Day 276: Nature Is My Sanctuary. 286

Day 277: I Am a Healer. 287

Day 278: All Disease and Discomfort Are Manifestations of
a Thought Pattern in My Mind. 288

Day 279: I Realign with My Desires Daily. 289

Day 280: I Choose My Words Wisely. 290

Day 281: I Actively Live My Highest Awareness. 291

Day 282: I Do Not Buy into Other People's Evaluations of Me. 292

Day 283: Everyone Is on His or Her Own Journey. 293

Day 284: I Explore My Fears So I Can Release Them for Good. 294

Day 285: The Universe Is Testing Me. 295

Day 286: I Ask for Feedback. 296

Day 287: I Get Out of the "But" Zone. 297

Day 288: Continuous Effort Gives Me Unlimited Potential. 298

Day 289: I Don't Have to See the Whole Path. I Take
One Step at a Time. 299

Day 290: I Am Clear with My Intentions. 300

Day 291: My Financial Abundance Is Reflected in What I See. 301

Day 292: I Detach from Social Vampires. 302

Day 293: I See the Reward in Taking Risks. 303

Day 294: I Create My Future by Envisioning It. 304

Day 295: I Allow Myself to Just Be Who I Am. 305

Day 296: Everyone Is Family. 306

Day 297: I Am Aware of My Stories. 307

Day 298: I Behave My Way to Success. 308

Day 299: I Take Time to Grieve. 309

Day 300: I Go for It. 310

Day 301: I Belong Here. 311

Day 302: I Do Not Judge Myself for Feeling My Feelings. 313

Day 303: One Day at a Time. 314

Day 304: I Nourish My Nudges. 315

Day 305: Everything Isn't Happening to Me. It's Happening for Me. 316

Day 306: I Avoid Emotional Reasoning. 317

Day 307: My Choices Are Not Forever or Final. 318

Day 308: I Ask What Lesson I Can Learn. 319

Day 309: Am I Failing Enough? 320

Day 310: I Gauge My Happiness by How Much Fun I Am Having. 321

Day 311: I Expect Great Results. 322

Day 312: I Am Succeeding at Life. 323

Day 313: I Am Not My Problems. 324

Day 314: I Don't Have to Be Happy All the Time. 325

Day 315: I Belong. 326

Day 316: When I Am Confident, Negativity Can't Get Me Down. 327

Day 317: My Body Knows How to Heal Itself. My Only Job
Is to Get Out of Its Way. 328

Day 318: I Live for the Moment. 329

Day 319: I Make Happiness My Favorite Habit. 330

Day 320: The Secret to Having It All Is Being Thankful for It All. 331

Day 321: I Focus on Results, Not Reasons. 332

Day 322: I Am in Touch with My Why. 333

Day 323: Everything Has a Honeymoon Stage. 334

Day 324: The Domino Effect of Being Kind Will Show Up
in Every Area of My Life. 335

Day 325: What I Do Today Has the Potential to Improve All
of My Tomorrows. 336

Day 326: I Am at Peace with Where I Am. 337

Day 327: I'm Over This Lesson. I Am Done. 338

Day 328: None of My Experiences Define Who I Am. 339

Day 329: I Can Change Directions. 340

Day 330: I Allow My Imagination to Explore Options for
Difficult Situations. 341

Day 331: I Believe Things Are Shifting in My Favor. 342

Day 332: Indecision Does Not Live in My Heart. 343

Day 333: I Compliment Myself Daily. 345

Day 334: I Am Always Growing and Needing New Teachers. 346

Day 335: Things Go Gray When I Forget to Play. 347

Day 336: I Protect My Energy. 348

Day 337: I Give Myself What I Needed Most as a Child. 349

Day 338: I Do My Part. 350

Day 339: I've Outgrown What I Once Needed to Grow Into. 351

Day 340: Growth Spurts Induce Fear, but There Is Nothing
to Be Afraid Of. 352

Day 341: They Are Not Judging Me. 353

Day 342: I Can't Change What I Don't Address. 354

Day 343: There Is No Reality, Only Perception. 355

Day 344: I Teach People How to Treat Me. 356

Day 345: Situations Don't Hurt. Expectations Do. 357

Day 346: There Is Plenty of Time. 358

Day 347: I Choose to Be Seen in My Radiant Totality,
and I Feel Safe and Supported Doing So. 359

Day 348: Some Things Fall Apart So They Can Come Back
Together at a Better Time. 360

Day 349: I Align My Thoughts with Love. 361

Day 350: Everything Is Relative. 362

Day 351: I Found My Happy. 363

Day 352: Instead of Trying to Get Attention, I Give It. 364

Day 353: I'm Not Afraid to Invest in My Dreams. 365

Day 354: I Am Selective with My Choices. 366

Day 355: Procrastination Is a Dead Desire. 367

Day 356: I Express Humility. 368

Day 357: I Don't Hang On to Moments. 369

Day 358: I Enjoy the Beauty of Becoming. 370

Day 359: There Are No Accidents. 371

Day 360: This Is Not My Practice Life. 372

Day 361: The Less I Know about "How," the Better. 373

Day 362: I Refuse to Stand In My Own Way. I Believe
in All I Can Be. 374

Day 363: My Future Starts Today. 376

Day 364: Whatever Will Be, Will Be. 375

Day 365: The Unknown Is Where I Can Dance Fully with Life. 378

Find Your Happy Daily Mantras Resources 379

Download the Free
Daily Mantra

"I AM PEACE" AUDIO MEDITATION

**WWW.PLAYWITHTHEWORLD.COM/DAILYMANTRAS/
FREEMEDITATION**

Introduction

Hello, Dear Reader,

I am so glad we are together on this journey. This is the revised and updated version of my original *Find Your Happy Daily Mantras.* I've teamed up with Beyond Words Publishing to create a powerful practice to help you align with happiness and fulfillment. There are new mantras, content, and tools in this book that will help you align with your best self. We've also created a card deck that goes with this book called the *Find Your Happy Daily Mantra Deck.* These tools can be used together or on their own.

The book you hold in your hands is a special project that was inspired by my first book. When I released *Find Your Happy: An Inspirational Guide to Loving Life to the Fullest,* readers all over the world reached out to share the impact it had on them. Many expressed their enthusiasm for the content and used it as a daily guide, often reading it again and again. But the real gift was the impact this book had on people who reached happiness while leaving depression, fear, and pain behind.

The transformational process has helped people who have suffered from depression, anxiety, self-doubt, and pain for years—even decades. It quickly became clear that I needed to take the work to the next level and create a daily practice. Much like it is for a daily devotional, the power of our healing capacity is in the daily action steps we take. The more positive action, the more positive results. This book in your hands is more than a self-help guide. It is a tool for recovery, providing hope and a path to freedom from pain.

Any recovery process requires a dedicated practice, which is why it became clear that using mantras, or daily meditations, is one of the most supportive and healing tools. I invite you to dive into this book with an open heart and self-compassion.

This book provides daily motivation to aid in your everlasting happiness. It will help you along your journey and gently guide you to new awareness and inner peace.

Several years ago, I was diagnosed with clinical depression. At the time, I was also suffering from eating disorders and addicted to drugs. I hit rock bottom, and my full surrender was the key to transformation. I turned my pain into purpose by sharing my journey of recovery. There is life after pain. It is possible. I am living proof.

Today I am happy, peaceful, and living my purpose. The main tool I use is daily mantras. These are powerful thoughts that can recondition our fear-based mind. The following pages serve as a 365-day practice to help turn happiness into a daily habit.

How to Use This Book

You are about to embark on a 365-day journey into wholeness, happiness, and your authentic self. Inside, I share my signature life coaching principles and the key to my own happiness.

Many people ask me how I overcame depression to live a happy and fulfilling life. Well, you are holding the instructions. The key to happiness is in the practice, and I've put it into a handy guide for you to enjoy.

The moment you chose to pick up this book, the healing began. You can read it in chronological order (one day at a time) or you can open to a random page and trust that is the message for you in the moment.

THE DAILY POWER MANTRA IN ACTION

I designed this book to maximize your healing by starting with a bold, powerful mantra. Each numbered day starts with the intention (or power mantra) that you focus on. Next you move onto a paragraph that is an overview of the situation. This will help you assess your experience and dive deeper into the message.

Once you finish with that, you move onto the Focused Intention (italicized paragraph), which is written in first person and can be read to yourself or out loud. The purpose for this section is to help you take the daily power mantra and put it into actual practice. Repeating these powerful words to yourself will solidify the healing and help return you to inner peace.

You will also discover full-page mantra pullouts throughout the book. These are designed like a meme to be used as additional visual motivation tools. You can snap a picture of the page to take with you anywhere, post to social media, send to your friends, or simply copy and print them so you can add them to own vision board. You can use them to help you feel connected to your authentic self.

THE POWER QUESTION

At the end of each daily mantra, I ask specific questions to help you take that mantra even deeper. I encourage you to have a special journal for the process and have fun answering the questions; they are strategically designed for maximum growth. You can write out your answer right there in your journal or answer the questions in your head during your meditation practice. Another option is to simply carry the question energetically with you throughout the day to help you align with your daily intention.

◇ ◇ ◇ ◇

Feel free to open the book each morning and throughout the day to receive the guidance in an instant. Like you would with an oracle deck, ask a question or lift up a concern to the Universe and then turn inward to be guided to a page. Trust that the message you open up to is the one for you to receive. I use this book in my coaching practice, and clients are continually amazed at how accurate the readings are. You will always get the mantra you are supposed to read.

This book was designed to be part of your overall wellness practice. I encourage you to set time aside each day to make happiness your favorite habit.

My wish is for you to use this book as daily inspiration, to help guide you to live your full potential. Each day is set up to deliver motivation for you to live a happy, peaceful, and fulfilling life.

Enjoy the adventure as you find your happy.

Love-filled hugs,

Shannon Kaiser

Day 1

I AM ABUNDANT AND SECURE.

Now is the time to take care of your resources and focus on what you have. It will not serve you to focus on what you lack. Giving time, money, or energy to an organization you care about will help you feel more abundant and, therefore, create an abundant flow of resources to you. You are always safe and protected.

◇ ◇ ◇ ◇

My worries and fears can sometimes get the best of me, but I know the truth is that I am always taken care of. The Universe has an abundant supply of everything I desire. I am protected and safe, and I allow myself to focus on what is good instead of what is not working. I release all lack mentality, the fear and inner critic, and turn to the abundance that is already apparent. I feel safe in the moment, and all my needs are always meet.

◇ ◇ ◇ ◇

In what ways am I abundant?

I am abundant Financially, and I Find even More ways to Make Money. The Universe always has a way of Protecting Me and Making sure My needs are Met. I have all that I need, and I am grateful to the Universe For the infinite abundance.

I AM BRAVE AND COURAGEOUS WITH MY HEART.

If you have any doubts or concerns, now is the time to release them. You may not feel ready to step into the next phase of your life, but you are more prepared than you realize. Let your courageous heart guide you.

◇ ◇ ◇ ◇

My heart is my compass to a happy life. If there is any area of my life I am unsatisfied with, now is the time for me to trust my heart to point me in the right direction.

My heart will always lead me to the solution that will overcome all challenges. I am brave in my undertaking as I move forward with confidence. All of the fear I feel will be removed when I listen to the pulse of my dreams in my heart.

◇ ◇ ◇ ◇

Where is my heart guiding me?

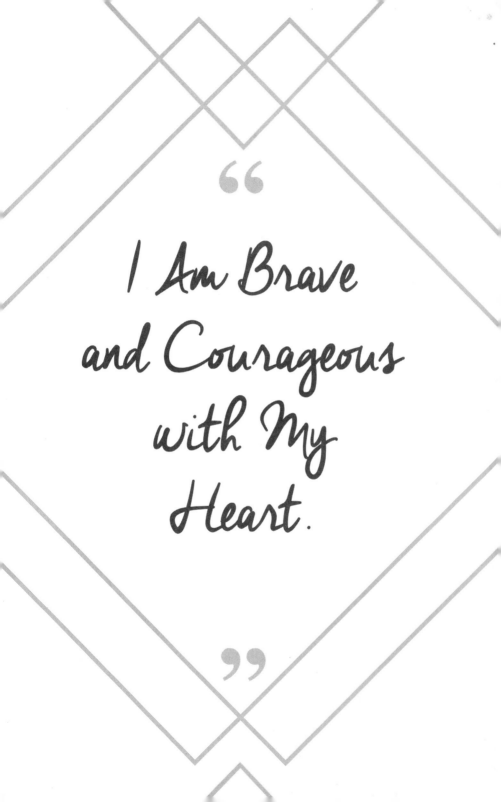

" "

I Am Brave
and Courageous
with My
Heart.

" "

I RELEASE ALL WORRY.
I CELEBRATE WHAT COULD GO RIGHT.

Positive thinking is important for you right now. Any troubling, negative thoughts could prevent you from reaching your goals. Instead of worrying about what could go wrong, start to celebrate what could go right.

◇ ◇ ◇ ◇

My worry does not serve me. It is like praying for what I don't want and hinders my ability to be happy. Instead of worry, I turn to trust. I know a plan is at play and I am being guided.

When I turn to my future self, I know everything always falls into place. If it is supposed to be part of my life plan, it will work out. I trust divine timing and allow my life to unfold naturally.

◇ ◇ ◇ ◇

What worry am I willing to release?

ALL MY NEEDS ARE ALWAYS MET.

There is no need for you to stay in any situation that no longer serves you. If an area of your life feels strained because you don't understand how it could possibly work out, you can turn to trust. Plenty of possibilities are available to you when you are open to receiving.

◇ ◇ ◇ ◇

I admit I sometimes get ahead of myself and become consumed with frustration. I release my need to know the outcome and align with my inner self.

I know I am taken care of and all my needs are met. When I fall into fear, I simply return to my true self by looking at all the things I do have.

◇ ◇ ◇ ◇

What am I grateful for today?

Day 5

ALL I DESIRE IS ON ITS WAY TO ME.

You've been working hard, but it may feel as if your goals are still out of reach. You might be feeling as if no matter how hard you try, you will never be as successful as everyone else, and it leaves you feeling hopeless. But this is a reminder that you've been working hard to reach your goals, and it would suit you to take time to rest and recover from all your hard work. This card is confirmation that what you want is on its way to you, and you don't have to work so hard to make it happen. Taking time to relax can help you become more productive and discover new ways to reach your goals.

◇ ◇ ◇ ◇

As I work toward my dreams, I realize that I don't have to work so hard. I can take time to relax. When I remove myself from the stress of trying to make things happen, I will be more productive because I am more balanced. The magic of living a fulfilling life is in celebrating my process as much as the outcome. The Universe is guiding me. I trust the signs that lead to my bigger picture.

◇ ◇ ◇ ◇

How can I relax today and take time
to nurture myself?

I AM OPEN AND WILLING TO LIVE MY LIFE IN NEW WAYS.

You may find yourself smack-dab in the middle of a huge transition. Perhaps something has happened that was unplanned and you are holding on to your past because it is all that you know. This time of change represents great growth for you, which will bring you blessings. It is essential you focus your attention on the new instead of holding on to the past. Old parts of your life are falling away; as this happens, invite in the new. Closed doors will always lead to new opportunities for growth and expansion. Your power is not in how the situation has played out but in how you proceed. Give thanks to the releasing of the old and welcome in the new with joy and excitement because your future is bright.

◇ ◇ ◇ ◇

Setbacks in life can be surprising opportunities for growth. Although this time of my life may be uncertain, I trust that my future self is guiding me. I am willing to see the silver lining and am open to living my life in refreshing new ways.

I believe everything happens for a reason, and I am willing to see the big picture in all difficult situations. As I move through my life transitions, I release the old and welcome new ways of living. All is for my greatest good.

◇ ◇ ◇ ◇

What new patterns and habits can I invite into my life?

Day 7

I TURN MY REACTION INTO COMPASSION.

It is easy to react to situations, especially when things aren't going the way you expected. But when we react, we block ourselves from receiving guidance and clear direction on how to move forward with grace and ease. The emotional outburst prevents us from feeling peace. The next time you find yourself reacting to a situation, take a moment to stop, take a deep breath, and turn your fear-based thoughts into more compassion. Simply ask yourself, "How can I see this situation with more love?" Let compassion rule your day by first being compassionate with yourself. It is natural to react to situations, but you can lessen your anger by being aware of your emotional outbursts. Then, simply practice balancing your emotions with more love and light.

◇ ◇ ◇ ◇

I choose to see all situations with more compassion. I am responsible for my outcome, and if there is a situation I do not like, I can lessen the frustration by seeing the situation from a new perspective. I let love lead the way as I choose to perceive everything with more kindness. As I send love and light to difficult situations, I can work through them much faster. I no longer react to frustrating circumstances; instead, I choose to be compassionate with myself and others.

◇ ◇ ◇ ◇

In what ways has my anger prevented me
from seeing the bigger picture?

EVERYTHING IS IN DIVINE ORDER.

Close your eyes and wish upon a star. The Universe is working out a divine plan for you, and all is in your favor. Feel hopeful and purposeful. Believe in your dreams, as they will come true for you. In this moment, you may feel paused or stuck. This is only temporary because circumstances are in the process of readjusting.

◇ ◇ ◇ ◇

There is a sacred timing to everything in my life. I release any concern that I am not where I need to be. I have made no mistakes, and where I am in this moment is perfect. When I start to worry about missing opportunities or when fears from the past creep in, I place my hand on my heart and repeat, "Everything is in divine order. I am right where I am supposed to be."

◇ ◇ ◇ ◇

What concerns am I willing to release?

Day 9

I AM SURROUNDED BY LOVE.
I AM PROTECTED.

You are so much stronger than you give yourself credit for. At times you may feel alone and unsafe, but today is a reminder that you are always protected and surrounded by love. Infinite energy surrounds you and wants you to succeed. You are more than willing and capable to overcome any current challenges. Instead of powering your way through it, shower the situation with love.

◇ ◇ ◇ ◇

The only thing keeping me from moving forward is my fear and recurring worry. The negative energy around me is not serving me, so I choose to release it and see the love surrounding me.

I surround the situations in my life that feel uncertain and unsafe with positivity. I let light in and know I am always protected.

◇ ◇ ◇ ◇

In what area of my life do I feel unsafe, and how can I let more love into this situation?

I GET WHAT I FOCUS ON.

Current situations may be consuming your life and sometimes make it difficult to focus on what the future holds. This card is a sign that you may be spending a lot of time focusing on how your current situation is not what you want or how you aren't where you hoped to be at this phase of your life. Instead of focusing on what isn't going well, recognize that you have the power to turn your attention around. This is a reminder that we get what we focus on. If what you want feels far away, instead of falling into despair and worry, turn your attention to focus on what you want. By doing this constantly, you will start to see more opportunities and get what you want faster.

◇ ◇ ◇ ◇

I turn my attention to focus on the feeling of what I want. I imagine myself in the situation and celebrate all that is. I focus my attention on feeling good and practice being in alignment with my desires.

◇ ◇ ◇ ◇

What have I been focusing on?

Day 11

THE FASTEST WAY TO FULFILLMENT IS TO LIVE MY VALUES.

If you feel stuck or trapped by certain situations that are happening in your life, it could be because you aren't expressing yourself fully. You have a unique value system that makes you who you are. You may value expressing yourself creatively, or you may crave more connection or exploration, but your current situation isn't allowing for such expressions to be utilized. This card is a reminder to be authentically you in order to be your happiest self. To remove the anxiety and depression caused from feeling stuck, you can apply your values into the situation and watch how your life transforms. The fastest way to feel more joy and love is to live what you value most.

◇ ◇ ◇ ◇

I am an expression of my unique set of values. I prioritize my happiness by focusing on the values that are essential for my own well-being. I do not settle or sacrifice my authentic truth; instead, I shine forward by being true to myself and expressing my honest, heartfelt values. My potential is lived when I express myself through living my values.

◇ ◇ ◇ ◇

What are my core values?

Day 12

I FEEL WITH MY HEART.

The heart can see and feel in ways your other senses cannot. Your heart is one of the most valuable tools you have in making your way through the world. Feeling with your heart is a spiritual concept that inspires you to make choices with your intuition and love instead of with your ego via your fear-based mind. Listen to the guidance that is within your heart: it is a feeling, a knowing, a deep understanding and intuitive sense that will never lead you astray. Always trust yourself and listen to your heart. Let it be the main way you feel.

◇ ◇ ◇ ◇

My heart is my compass, and I listen to it and feel with it daily. My intuition is part of my greater understanding, and I trust the guidance I feel within. My heart is my companion and will lead me into the right situation every time.

◇ ◇ ◇ ◇

What message has my heart been giving me lately?

Day 13

I AM OPEN TO THE THINGS
I DO NOT KNOW YET.

You are always changing and growing, and in the pursuit of reaching new goals, you may feel frustrated, as if your efforts aren't paying off. Realize that the journey to reaching your dreams is more important than actually manifested outcomes because of the learning that happens in the space in between. Instead of pushing against what is and letting your frustration overtake you, simply surrender fully and repeat the mantra "I am open to the things I don't yet know." Let yourself learn the way as you move forward, and you will relax into the gentle flow of life. There are abundant resources available to you, but you need to be willing to learn new ways of approaching old situations.

◇ ◇ ◇ ◇

I understand that there are things out of my control, and my only job is to surrender my need to control them. I release my need to know how things will work out and instead relax into the unknown. I am open and willing to learn new things, and I pay attention to the guidance I receive. I am aware that there are things I don't know yet, and it is because it is not time to know them. Time is on my side, and everything will be revealed at the right time and in the right place.

◇ ◇ ◇ ◇

What circumstance have I been trying to control?

ABUNDANCE AND JOY ARE MY BIRTHRIGHT.

There is no need for you to be in fear. Joy is natural to you. Stop holding on to negative and fearful thoughts. There is no need to worry, as you were born to be happy. Instead of giving your attention to things that bother you, allow them to fall away. Harmony will soon come to you, as joy and abundance are your birthright.

◇ ◇ ◇ ◇

I am not my worries or concerns. I am so much bigger than any dilemmas in my life. I choose to see the good in each situation, and I focus my attention on all that is well. I am joyful and connected to my truth.

Joy is my natural state of well-being, and I align with it daily. I always have everything I need, and happiness flows to me.

◇ ◇ ◇ ◇

What does abundance mean to me?

Day 15

I SEE THE LIGHT AND LOVE IN OTHERS.

Other people may do things you don't understand. Everyone has their own opinion, way of doing things, and clear point of view, so just because others may differ does not mean they are wrong. There is great understanding in the differences and the contrasts of life. Instead of lashing out with anger or trying to get others to see your perspective, simply flood them energetically with love and light. The divine light in you is also in them, as everyone on planet Earth is connected through the human experience. See others as your own family and you will feel more at peace.

◇ ◇ ◇ ◇

I stop trying to understand people and instead let them be who they are, as they are. I will no longer participate in the drama of the world, and I refuse to let negative actions pull me in. Instead, I send love and light to others, and I see and acknowledge the light within us all.

◇ ◇ ◇ ◇

Who can I send love and light to?

WHEN I FOLLOW MY PASSIONS, MY PURPOSE IS REVEALED.

You might be trying too hard to find your purpose. If you are overthinking and struggling to find the answers, you could be blocking the answers from coming. Instead of thinking your way into your purpose, try to feel your way into it. Ask yourself what feels right as you explore new opportunities and ventures. Finding your purpose is a process that derives from your heart.

◇ ◇ ◇ ◇

I am in the process, and I trust my plan is being revealed to me. When I focus on what brings me joy, I live with purpose, which brings me clarity.

I align with what feels good and step away from limiting beliefs that tell me I have to have my purpose all figured out. My life is perfect the way it is, and I am joyfully expressing myself.

◇ ◇ ◇ ◇

What brings me the most joy today?

Day 17

WHEN I CLEAN UP MY THOUGHTS, I CLEAN UP MY LIFE.

Just like a magnet that attracts its likeness, the laws of the Universe state that your thoughts create your reality. If you are dissatisfied with an area of your life, it is essential you take responsibility and consider your recent and current thoughts. When you clean up your thoughts, you clean up your life. Remember that you attract to you that which occurs.

◇ ◇ ◇ ◇

I am accountable for all that I experience. I choose loving, kind, and supportive thoughts, which help align me with my truth. I solve all situations with love. My current reality is a result of my previous thoughts. If I want to change my situation, I start by changing my thoughts about it. I release the negative hold of fear and align with my truth and love. I attract good things to me.

◇ ◇ ◇ ◇

Where can I take responsibility for my outcome?

EVERYTHING I NEED IS INSIDE OF ME.

You may worry you don't have what you need to get to where it is you want to go. But today is a reminder you have everything you will ever need to reach your goals. Your future is unfolding in the present moment, and it is essential that you hold positive thoughts. You are more capable and willing than you give yourself credit for. Instead of focusing on how it can't work, turn your attention to opportunities in front of you. When you are open to receiving guidance, there are plenty of ways to reach your desired outcome.

◇ ◇ ◇ ◇

I am strong, capable, and focused. I release my need to have it all figured out, and I go inward to reveal the best path forward. I am always being guided to learn, grow, and trust more. Today, I align with my truth and the desires of my heart. I take one step at a time, and the path is revealed to me. I always have what I need to get to where I want to go. I learn the way on the way.

◇ ◇ ◇ ◇

Where can I give myself more credit
for a job well done?

Day 19

I BELIEVE IN THE GOOD OF MANKIND.

For the next two weeks, turn your attention inward and stop looking outside to the media and for news of current events. Life is happening all around you, but when you turn to negative coverage, it projects a one-sided view. The world is a kind and loving place, and when you can align with love, you will see evidence of this.

◇ ◇ ◇ ◇

I release my attention from negative current events and focus on the qualities of mankind that are good. I see beauty in people, and I smile with joy. I give people the benefit of the doubt and release harsh judgment and criticism. I know everyone is doing the best they can, and together we can all choose love and peace.

◇ ◇ ◇ ◇

What qualities of mankind do I love?

WHAT I SEEK IS ON ITS WAY TO ME.

At any given moment, you have a choice. You can focus on what is not yet here, or you can turn your attention to what is working in your life. Focus actively on the good qualities of your life and you will begin to see evidence of your desires in motion. What you desire also desires you, so it is important to hold faith that what you want is on its way, because it is.

◇ ◇ ◇ ◇

I align with my highest good, and all I desire is on its way to me. What I seek is seeking me. Even though I cannot see evidence of my outcome, I hold faith I will get what I need at the right time for me. My desires are in full bloom, and I hold faith they will come true soon.

◇ ◇ ◇ ◇

How can I focus more on what is working
instead of what is not?

I RECOGNIZE AND HONOR THE LIGHT INSIDE OF ME.

There is a duality inside every person. An ego-based thought process—one of fear, darkness, and negative energy—and a loving, heart-based perception of kindness, compassion, and peace. It is impossible to live a life free of one without the other. Instead of judging others or lashing out with anger, look at the anger within yourself. Diminish your negative energy by focusing on the love and light within you. Let the love rise to the surface with more attention on kindness. Choose to see the light within you by speaking kindly to yourself and being compassionate to yourself and others.

◇ ◇ ◇ ◇

There is a light so bold, bright, and courageous inside of me, and I am not afraid to shine it. I let myself feel the love within and honor the light that is me. I am an example of what is possible when you choose love over fear, and I stand in my bright light to help others shine bright too.

◇ ◇ ◇ ◇

In what ways have I been afraid to
shine my own light?

THE RIGHT CHOICE IS THE CHOICE THAT FEELS EXPANSIVE AND JOYFUL.

You may be at a crossroads and wonder which choice is the best one for you. Should you stay, or should you go? Should you invest or save? When we focus on our choices and overanalyze them, wondering which one will be right, we can become paralyzed with fear. Instead of obsessing over a future outcome that has yet to reveal itself, focus inward on the choice that feels the most expansive. Which choice feels joyful and loving? This is the right choice for you because it is an extension of your authentic self, and that will always guide you correctly. If you are worried or in fear, that is a choice derived from ego and your anxious head. Instead, drop from your head to your heart and step forward in the choice that feels the most expansive and joyful.

◇ ◇ ◇ ◇

All my choices help me grow. I cannot make a wrong choice when I align with my truth. I choose what feels good and expansive for this is always the choice for my highest good. Instead of worrying about the outcome, I turn my focus to the energetic alignment of joy. I focus on the choice that feels good and light filled, the choice with possibilities and potential.

◇ ◇ ◇ ◇

What choice feels most expansive and joy-filled?

Day 23

I AM NOT ALONE.

Although you may feel alone, you are never truly by yourself. Your heart, support system, guides, higher power, and higher self are always with you, gently guiding you to peace and understanding. If you feel lonely, turn your focus to the love around you. You are protected and cared for, now and always.

◇ ◇ ◇ ◇

I am never truly alone. I may feel lonely, but I know I am surrounded by love. I trust the silence as it allows me to go inward to express my truth from my heart. I am safe, protected, and secure. I am never alone.

◇ ◇ ◇ ◇

Who can I reach out to for companionship?

MY STRESS IS TRYING TO TELL ME SOMETHING.

You may be overwhelmed and working too hard. If you feel stressed, this is an indication of imbalance and your life is not flowing. Instead of trying to get it all done and work hard to make something happen, consider a more playful, fun approach. When you add joy to your routine, your stress levels go down.

◇ ◇ ◇ ◇

I remove all unnecessary worry and tasks from my life. I choose to focus on adding more fun-loving energy to my stressful situations. This helps me get out of my own way, so I can be more productive and playful.

◇ ◇ ◇ ◇

Where can I add more play into my life?

Day 25

REGARDLESS OF THE OUTCOME, I AM TAKEN CARE OF.

You need not worry about the resolution of the current situation. Instead of trying to solve the problem with sheer force, trust you will get exactly what you need. No matter what the outcome of this uncertain situation is, you are taken care of.

◇ ◇ ◇ ◇

All of my needs are met. I am full of love, and my attention is on the present moment. For in this moment, I am secure and have everything I need. No matter what the outcome, I know it will be for my greater good.

◇ ◇ ◇ ◇

What negative belief can I let go of
regarding an uncertain situation?

I CELEBRATE LIFE'S LITTLE VICTORIES.

Are you worrying too much? If so, you are probably focused on the outcome instead of enjoying the process. If you were to stop and reflect, you would see how extraordinary you truly are and how far you have already come. Celebrate where you are today, for you are brilliantly beautiful in this moment. You are doing a great job.

◇ ◇ ◇ ◇

I am proud of how far I have come. I celebrate my life and all of the little victories along the way. I have goals I am working toward, but I am happy to be where I am. I accept myself and embrace the process fully.

◇ ◇ ◇ ◇

What little victories am I proud of?

NEEDING SOMEONE IS NOT A WEAKNESS. IT IS AN ACT OF SELF-LOVE.

Relying on someone else is not a weakness. You have been strong for so long, and there is no need to have your guard up. Instead of protecting your heart, consider a more vulnerable approach and let love in. By showing someone that you need them, you respect yourself more.

◇ ◇ ◇ ◇

It is safe to show the real me. I need help and support, and I am open to receiving this support from loved ones. I show up for myself when I allow myself to need others. I am strong and independent, but needing someone is essential for my well-being. I let others in.

◇ ◇ ◇ ◇

Where can I ask for help, and who can I let in?

Day 28

I AM ONLY ISOLATED BY MY ILLUSION. I PERCEIVE OTHERS WITH LOVE.

You may feel left out or as if others don't fully understand you. Do not take it personally or feel isolated. Other people are in fear and afraid of what they don't understand. When you live a light-filled life, one where you are actively aligned with love, you make choices with your heart. This is an unknown way of living for many people, but you are here to live in your greatness. Do not shy away from who you truly are. Instead of feeling alone, see that your life and calling are grand. Perceive others with love and continue on your path. Let your heart guide you and you will never be disappointed.

◇ ◇ ◇ ◇

I choose to see others as love and light. Other people cannot harm me with their opposing interests, opinions, or conflicting views. I stand in my truth and see others with love. I am love, and I send my love to others. All is in right order, and all is well when I choose to perceive the world with light and love.

◇ ◇ ◇ ◇

Who is hurting that I can send love to?

THE PRESENT MOMENT IS
ALL THAT MATTERS.

You may feel overwhelmed with specific situations and outcomes in your life. Now is not the time to worry or try to control the outcome. Look at where you are holding on to expectations and release them. When you feel overwhelmed by life's circumstances, know that fearing for the future will not serve you. All we have is this moment, so turn your attention to the now and your fear will subside.

◇ ◇ ◇ ◇

I understand some things are out of my control, and I am okay with that. I release all fear from my past and anxiety for the future. Instead, I return to the moment and know that things are always as they should be.

◇ ◇ ◇ ◇

What expectations am I ready to release?

CLUTTER IS A BYPRODUCT OF INDECISION. I REMOVE ALL EXTRA STUFF FROM MY LIFE.

If you are overwhelmed with a situation, consider looking at the clutter in your life. Everything is connected, and clutter in your home is a byproduct of indecision.

Clutter can be physical or emotional. Now is the time to remove all extra stuff and welcome in new energy that is aligned with your truth.

◇ ◇ ◇ ◇

My thoughts are pure, my energy is light, and I am clutter-free. I take time to remove everything that no longer serves me. This includes people, products, ideas, and beliefs. By releasing what no longer works, I make room for what does.

◇ ◇ ◇ ◇

What can I remove from my life?

"

The First Step
to Improving the
World Is to Improve
Myself.

"

THE FIRST STEP TO IMPROVING THE WORLD IS TO IMPROVE MYSELF.

You may be focusing a great deal of time and energy on the world's state of affairs. Perhaps you are giving your attention to what is not going well. When we pay attention to the media, it will seem like the world is falling apart, but there is great good in this world, and it starts within each of us. Instead of focusing on how hopeless or helpless you feel, choose to see yourself as a powerful change-maker. You do have the power to make a difference by being true to yourself and proactively improving your own life. When you stand in your own light, you inspire others to do the same, and this simple act will help to uplift the entire world.

◇ ◇ ◇ ◇

I stop focusing on the negative aspects of this world and instead turn inward to focus on my own negative attitudes. I am gentle and kind to myself as I heal and grow. I choose to see myself with love and kindness, and this seemingly simple act will help to improve the entire world. When I shine more light, it helps uplift the world with more positive energy.

◇ ◇ ◇ ◇

What habit or negative belief has been holding me back?

Day 32

I RELEASE MY NEED TO GET THERE.

Life is not a race. There is no final destination where you can arrive. Each goal you create is part of a bigger life plan and process. Instead of focusing so much on the outcome, this is a gentle reminder to have more fun on the journey. The process is part of the goal, and it is where the magic can happen.

◇ ◇ ◇ ◇

I will look back one day and realize the little things were the real, tangible parts of my life. So I will enjoy the journey just as much as the destination. I am in the process of my life and allow it to be what it is. I give up my need to manipulate my outcome or force myself to get there. Instead, I have fun along the way and play in the journey.

◇ ◇ ◇ ◇

What outcome have I been holding on to?

Day 33

INSTEAD OF FOCUSING ON THE ANGER, I FOCUS ON HEALING THE PAIN.

There are times when the person who is hurting you the most is yourself, and you may not even realize it. You may be mad at a situation or person who has caused you emotional angst, and you're having a hard time of letting go of that anger. It's hard to understand why you would allow such a negative emotion to consume you, but don't beat yourself up over it. Sometimes we hold on to anger because it is all we have left of a person or situation that is no longer in our life. This is a natural reaction to loss even if it is not very helpful for your mind, body, and soul. Instead of holding on to the anger, turn your attention to healing the pain. Anger is manifested pain that just needs to be soothed with more love and attention. You can heal yourself by focusing on sending more love in the direction of the pain.

◇ ◇ ◇ ◇

I release the pain that I am holding in my heart. I let go of the anger because I know that it is no longer serving me. My internal angst is a reflection of unhealed wounds that need more love and focus. As I seek inward to comfort my pain, as I move through my emotional frustration, I can see that anger is no longer needed. I forgive all involved and instead focus all my energy on healing the pain.

◇ ◇ ◇ ◇

What painful situation or person has made me angry?
How can I focus on healing that pain?

Day 34

I RESPECT EXPIRATION DATES.

You may be feeling trapped or hung up on an event or relationship that belongs in the past. Sometimes we hold on to negative feelings about past events because we wish that the situations had not changed. Conditions for our lives are ever changing, and often that means things come to an end. Grasping tightly onto an expired situation can only cause heartache. It is time to release your grip and respect the situation for what it was. When relationships, jobs, living situations, or other life events end, something else is always waiting in the wings for you to give your attention.

◇ ◇ ◇ ◇

I let go of events and relationships that no longer serve me. Everything has its season, and one season has ended, but this is no reason for despair. My reluctance to move on changes into confidence that something that is right for me is on its way. I thank the situations that have expired for the service they did in my life, and I reset my mind and heart to receive what comes next.

◇ ◇ ◇ ◇

What relationship or situation has expired
and needs to be let go of in my life?

Day 35

MY LIFE IS A COURAGEOUS, CREATIVE ADVENTURE.

Your life is what you make of it. Everything you are currently experiencing is part of your choices, perceptions, and what you have previously focused on. If you are in a situation that isn't as fulfilling as you would like, focus on how courageous you are and how far you have come. In each and every moment, you have an opportunity to create the life you truly want. Your life is a creative adventure that can only be designed by you. Let inspiration and creativity pull you forward. Anything and everything you want is possible when you tap into your courageous heart and let it pull you forward.

◇ ◇ ◇ ◇

My life is full of joy, inspiration, love, and light. I know that every action I take helps create my ideal future. I focus fully on what I want and embrace the journey as I become more of who I want to be. My life is a courageous, creative adventure.

◇ ◇ ◇ ◇

What part of my life can I look at more
as an adventure?

Day 36

EVERY NEXT LEVEL OF MY LIFE WILL DEMAND A DIFFERENT VERSION OF ME.

You did it. You are living your dream. You got what you set out to get, so why doesn't it feel the way you thought it would? It could be that you are still functioning as a version of you that is no longer serving your current life; it takes time to adjust to our new selves. The reality is that many dreams are not meant to be long lasting; often they are stepping-stones to bigger, longer-lasting goals. Sometimes we go for a dream, and it manifests to give us tools, learning, and lessons that will then lead us to an even bigger dream that is part of our life plan. The purpose is to focus on living a life dedicated to your dreams, and as you show up for each new dream, you will be asked to bring a new version of you forward. Each dream helps you become more of who you really are.

◇ ◇ ◇ ◇

I am proud of who I have become, and now is the time to step up to the next level of my life. I show up with confident joy, and I am proud of my manifested dreams. My life is always unfolding, and I show up to each phase more committed and connected to my true self. I express my authentic truth in each level of my life as I commit to showing up fully as a refreshed version of me.

◇ ◇ ◇ ◇

What version of me does my next level of life require?

Day 37

EVERYTHING HAPPENS AT THE RIGHT TIME AND PLACE.

Imagine, if you will, that you are a farmer, working really hard to till to your soil. The more you plant, the more abundance and opportunities you will have in the future. It is important to look at your life in the same manner; everything that happens has a particular season, and for each season, there is always a reason. Recognize that everything will manifest at the right time and in the right place. If things aren't manifesting in the way you hoped, keep tending to your farm and planting more seeds. The more work you put into your situation, the more beautiful the outcome.

◇ ◇ ◇ ◇

I know that my hard work will pay off. There is no endpoint to the amount of abundance and opportunities I can receive—it just comes back to timing. I trust that everything has a special time and place, and all is in the right order. I continue to plant seeds and watch my dreams grow.

◇ ◇ ◇ ◇

What is the reason for my current season?

THE MORE I KNOW MYSELF, THE MORE I CAN BE MYSELF.

The more you know yourself, the more you can be yourself, and the more you can be yourself, the easier it is for you to feel comfortable in your own skin and shine more light. The more you can express your true self, the more you inspire those around you to be themselves. There is a ripple effect to being true to yourself, but it starts with knowing yourself. Instead of focusing so much on the outside world and getting more things or reaching more goals, focus inward on knowing yourself better. When you truly know yourself, you will reach your desires with less effort and without strain. Let yourself be who you really are by being honest and forthcoming with yourself.

◇ ◇ ◇ ◇

I am comfortable in my skin. I know who I am and work toward learning more about myself each day. I understand that everything is presented in life for me to learn and grow from, but it all comes back to me and my reactions or acceptance of it. Instead of reacting, condemning, or judging, I will see myself as the beautiful light that I am. I am amazing just as I am, and it's time for me to be true to myself, starting with knowing myself even more.

◇ ◇ ◇ ◇

How well do I really know me?

FORGIVENESS ISN'T ABOUT FREEING ME FROM MY PAST. IT IS ABOUT OPENING UP MY FUTURE.

Be honest with yourself and look at relationships where you are harboring resentment. Perhaps you have tried to forgive but struggled to release the situation from your life. Maybe you feel it is unspiritual to be angry, so you try to pretend everything is okay. Allow yourself to feel the feelings. This will let them move through you, and you will release them for good. Then forgiveness can set in.

◇ ◇ ◇ ◇

I give myself permission to feel my feelings. I allow them to move through me. I look at all areas of my life and clean out emotional clutter by releasing resentment. My actions are guided with love. I am letting go of my past, so I can free myself up to new opportunities in my future. I forgive.

◇ ◇ ◇ ◇

Who can I forgive today?

Day 40

IT'S NOT ABOUT WHERE I AM GOING BUT WHO I BECOME.

You've been putting a lot of effort and attention into the outcome. Trying to make things happen before they are fully ready to manifest. If you feel frustrated or angry, it could be because your goal has not yet come true. Instead of focusing so much on the destination, turn your attention to the journey. Who you are today is more important than who you will become when you reach your goal, because today is where the learning is. You are learning valuable lessons to help you become the person who can receive the wish you truly desire. Who you are becoming now is worth celebrating. The here and now is all you have—be present and celebrate all that is.

◇ ◇ ◇ ◇

It is not about the destination but the journey, and I am fully present for mine. I celebrate who I am and make myself available for learning new lessons. I create my own reality by aligning with love and light. When I focus forward with clarity, I make my present circumstances more balanced. Everything is always changing, and I am growing more into who I want to be, but today matters more than my tomorrow. I happily accept where I am and appreciate all that I am becoming.

◇ ◇ ◇ ◇

What current situation can I celebrate?

Day 41

I DON'T TAKE MYSELF TOO SERIOUSLY. I SEE THE LIGHTHEARTEDNESS IN THIS MOMENT.

Life can be difficult, and it is even harder when you take everything seriously. Today's opportunity is to bring more joy into this moment. Seriousness has its own time and place, but consider bringing more lighthearted energy to the situation causing you the most distress. This will give way to new opportunities to solve the problem.

◇ ◇ ◇ ◇

I smile more and let light in. I may be taking myself too seriously, which does not serve me. Instead of powering my way through this troubling situation, I smile and invite more lighthearted energy into my life. I am happy and free.

◇ ◇ ◇ ◇

Where can I lighten up?

Day 12

EVERYTHING'S GOING TO BE ALL RIGHT. IT ALWAYS WORKS OUT IN THE END.

If you look back on your life, you may see proof that everything always works out in the end. If you are in a situation causing you extreme stress, recognize it is not the end. Dive into the experience and you will come out on the other side with grace and ease.

◇ ◇ ◇ ◇

I am worry-free and supported by my higher self. I choose to see all situations as opportunities for expansive growth. I know things are falling into place, and everything always works out in the end. I trust my internal guidance as I move forward.

◇ ◇ ◇ ◇

What past experiences have worked out in my favor?

LIFE IS ABOUT DETOURS.
I TAKE THE ROAD LESS TRAVELED
AND EMBRACE THE UNKNOWN.

You may feel as though your life is off track, but you are more on track than you have ever been. Your life is a creative exploration of arriving at your true self. Trust the process and be open to glorious detours. The road in front of you is paved by your own adventure. Embrace the unknown.

◇ ◇ ◇ ◇

I am open to taking new paths to solve old problems. I am fearless. I face forward with confidence and jump into my life with wide-open arms. My heart is the compass. I take detours and know they lead me to a greater awareness of my place in this world. My life is an adventure I navigate with love.

◇ ◇ ◇ ◇

How can I step out of my comfort zone today?

MY DREAMS ARE THE SIGNATURE TO MY POTENTIAL.

Your dreams matter, and so do you. You have inspiration that comes to you daily, but you may be ignoring it. Instead of worrying about how or when it can happen, focus on taking clear steps to make it happen. You are in charge of your own life, and the outcome is in your own hands. This is empowering because whatever you think and believe, you can achieve. If you want more abundance, focus on feeling abundant within. If you want to find your soul mate, focus on giving yourself the love you so desire. Everything you want is on its way to you, but it can't come to you if you aren't taking action on your dreams daily. Commit daily to your dreams for they are the signature to your potential.

◇ ◇ ◇ ◇

My dreams matter, and I commit to taking action on them daily. I know that my life gets better through change, and I embrace the new opportunities coming to me because I know they are direct results of my previous efforts.

◇ ◇ ◇ ◇

What is something I have always wanted to do but haven't given myself permission to do?

Day 45

I TRUST MY INTUITION.

Your inner guidance system is an intricate orchestra of love and passion. When you tune in to your own wisdom, you will never fail. Trust yourself, as you know yourself on a soul level, deeper than anyone else in the world. Now is the time to listen deeply to the voice within. It is leading you to where you truly long to go.

◇ ◇ ◇ ◇

I trust myself. My inner voice is always speaking to me, and it feels expansive. I align with my true intuition, which is light filled and joyful. My purpose is to follow my heart, and I trust the voice within. My intuition is my best mentor as I move forward. I listen to its honest reflection of my truth.

◇ ◇ ◇ ◇

What has my intuition been trying to tell me?

I AM NOT DAMAGED OR WOUNDED. THERE IS NOTHING WRONG WITH ME.

The situations from your past have not damaged you. They have taught you lessons about life and your true awareness of self. Your current circumstances are not a result of you being unfixable. You are stronger and more capable then you give yourself credit for. Dive forward with confidence and whole-heart love.

◇ ◇ ◇ ◇

I am a warrior of my past. I am an overcomer and survivor of all that life has thrown at me. I am not damaged. There is nothing to fix. I am a perfect child of the Universe, and I am full of love. I shine my light forward with confidence and courage. I matter. I am whole.

◇ ◇ ◇ ◇

Where do I feel broken?
What steps will I take to release this internal pain?

ANYTHING I GIVE MY ATTENTION TO WILL FLOURISH AND GROW.

Pay attention to where you focus your thoughts. What you see is a result of where you have been putting your emotional energy. If there is an area of your life you are dissatisfied with, look back to your recent and current thoughts about that situation. Turn your focus to what you want, and watch it flourish and grow.

◇ ◇ ◇ ◇

I am responsible for all I experience. I always align with my loving light and focus on what I want with joy and ease. I release all worry and spend my time creating my joy-filled reality. When I focus on what I want, it flourishes and comes to me.

◇ ◇ ◇ ◇

What area of my life can I give more
loving attention to?

Day 48

SELF-LOVE IS NOT ABOUT HOW I LOOK OR WHAT I DO—IT'S ABOUT HOW I LIVE.

You are putting a lot of pressure on yourself to look and be a certain way. You may be overcritical and blaming yourself for things that aren't even your fault. When we lack self-love, we tend to feel more guilt and pressure. We often focus on our insecurities instead of our strengths. You drew this mantra today because your critical mind has been obsessing and running the show, which has prevented you from seeing how amazing, beautiful, and wonderful you really are. Instead of focusing on how you look and the physical problems you think are hindering you, recognize that self-love is about how you live. Focus more on how you feel and live a life that feels good on the inside, which will, in turn, manifest itself on the outside.

◇ ◇ ◇ ◇

How I feel is more important than how I look. Instead of focusing on my insecurities, I make an active choice to align my heart and thoughts with love. I know that self-love is about taking steps daily to care for myself and accept myself as I am. I am a beautiful child of the Universe, and the Universe makes no mistakes. I accept myself and choose to live my life with intention, joy, and ease.

◇ ◇ ◇ ◇

How can I show up for myself more today?

I THINK FROM MY HEART.

Your rational mind works extra hard throughout your life. It may analyze everything and try you in order to make smart, calculated moves forward. But in the past, it may have kept you in situations that no longer served you.

Now is the time to think from your heart. You may be used to feeling with your heart and trusting the guidance, but thinking with your heart means aligning your head and heart into one. Your ego and mind need not be separate. Your fear can turn into love when you think from your heart.

◇ ◇ ◇ ◇

My heart has guidance for me, and I trust the process it reveals. I think with my heart as it shows me the correct next action. I am always safe and protected because my head and heart are aligned.

◇ ◇ ◇ ◇

How can I align my head and heart to help me move through my current situation?

IT IS OKAY TO CHANGE MY MIND.

You need not stay in any situation that causes you pain. At any given moment, you have the power to make another choice. If an area of your life is bringing you down, consider changing your mind.

Your life is an ever-expansive journey, and changing your mind is part of the big picture. Instead of resisting change or holding on to the old, free yourself up from the emotional confines by making a different decision.

◇ ◇ ◇ ◇

I am comfortable with my choices and position in life. I change my mind with confidence and know I am being guided to new opportunities. When I quiet my fear-based voice, I can feel my truth from my heart. I am guided into new directions, and it is safe to change my mind.

◇ ◇ ◇ ◇

Where can I change my mind?

Day 51

EMBRACE THE SPACE BETWEEN WHERE I AM AND WHERE I WANT TO BE.

Slow down. You may be too focused on the outcome. When you can add more love into this moment, you will embrace the process more. Instead of racing to meet your goal, savor all the sweet moments along the way. Through the process, you become who you are meant to be. Allow yourself to be more present in the journey, which will help you grow.

◇ ◇ ◇ ◇

I am in no rush. I simply savor the sweet moments of my life and trust the divine unfolding of everything in its right time and place. I look forward to learning new things as I grow more into my best self.

◇ ◇ ◇ ◇

What am I learning on the way to
reaching my goal?

MY BELIEFS DO NOT DEFINE ME. I AM WILLING TO SEE OTHER PERSPECTIVES WITHOUT JUDGMENT.

You may get frustrated because others don't see things the way you do. Let go of the need to prove yourself right. Instead, see the diversity of ideas as a gift. Everyone is entitled to their own beliefs and opinions, including you. But do not mistake your views as a definition of who you are. You are so much more than your own beliefs, so consider a more open-minded approach to life as you move forward.

◇ ◇ ◇ ◇

I am aligned with my inner light, and my light is truth. I do not have a need to prove myself right. They have opinions and beliefs that help color the contrast of the world. There is no wrong or right. We all belong.

Instead of defining myself or judging others by my opinions, I see us all as love and light. We are all connected by our diverse thoughts and ideals.

◇ ◇ ◇ ◇

Do I want to be right, or would I rather be happy?

MY INNER CHILD WANTS TO PLAY.

Most of your energy has been consumed with life's demands and adult responsibilities. But there is a more playful approach to life, and that approach is already within you. Your inner child has been with you all along but has felt pushed aside. Your inner child is the true you, the one who is playful, compassionate, curious, and full of love. Return to your true self and allow your inner child to come out and play.

◇ ◇ ◇ ◇

I turn inward and allow my inner child to come forth. My joy-filled, expressive self deserves to be heard. My inner child has a message for me, and I listen to the wisdom. Each day, I return to my true self by allowing my inner child to come out and play.

◇ ◇ ◇ ◇

What did I love to do as a child that I can do today?

THIS IS THE LIFE I WANT TO LIVE.

You get to create the life you want to live. By focusing on what you want and taking action daily, you can create a new reality for yourself and loved ones. This life is for you to live your dreams and your full potential. Do not shy away by leaning into fear; instead, stand tall and proud of the life you are living. It is your creative adventure and masterpiece.

◇ ◇ ◇ ◇

I am proud of who I am and all that I've been through. I've worked hard to be me, and it has paid off. The more me I show, the more my life will flow, and I am honored to be me. I am proud of myself and see the great things I have to offer this world. I love myself and my life. This is the life I want to live.

◇ ◇ ◇ ◇

Am I who I want to be?

Day 55

I LISTEN TO THE GUIDANCE
COMING MY WAY.

Your ears are valuable resources to help you overcome any and all situations. If you are in circumstances that do not feel good, instead of overthinking or overanalyzing, simply perk up your ears and listen more intently. Learn how to use your ears as eyes, listening to the deep rhythm of the world. The sounds can give you a greater understanding of the truth. Just as nature works together with the sounds and sights, you too can propel your life forward by using all your senses with more intention. The same way the wave crashes and folds into the sand, you hear the wave as you see the wave. The two work together to make your experience more rich and fulfilling. Use this same concept to solve troubled situations in your life.

◇ ◇ ◇ ◇

I use my ears to listen to solutions so I can solve my problems with more confidence and clarity. I see clearly when I stop overthinking and instead listen more to those around me. I am comfortable in the silence, for there is guidance that I can gain.

◇ ◇ ◇ ◇

What guidance have I recently heard
but keep ignoring?

Day 56

I WITNESS SITUATIONS
WITHOUT JUDGMENT.

When you judge situations, people, and experiences, you prevent yourself from being present in your life. Judgment is a stand-in for lack of love. Instead of observing situations with a need to fix, solve, or prove others wrong, consider a more compassionate approach. You can do this by stepping back and witnessing your life as if you are watching it on a movie screen. This allows you to see the big picture.

◇ ◇ ◇ ◇

I am free of judgment and self-blame. I watch all situations in my life without a need to criticize, fix, or blame. I am accountable for what I see, but I do not take it personally. I am free of all judgment and witness all situations with love.

◇ ◇ ◇ ◇

What situation have I recently been overcritical about?
How can I send more love to this experience?

I AM HURTING, AND THAT IS OKAY.

You need not hide your pain, nor do you need to push it away. Feeling hurt is part of living a balanced life. You may be on a spiritual path and feel as if you shouldn't be hurting or in pain. But this couldn't be further form the truth. True self-awareness comes from embracing all emotions as they come up.

Allow yourself to be in the pain as you feel it. In time, the pain will remove itself from your life. Be kind to yourself. It takes time to heal. There is no expiration date on healing. Time will give you what you need.

◇ ◇ ◇ ◇

I am hurting, but that is part of the process of healing. It is okay to feel these emotions. I choose to dive into this pain rather than numbing myself or running away. My pain has a message for me, and I can learn from this experience. I embrace all of life's experiences and feel them fully.

◇ ◇ ◇ ◇

Where in my life have I blocked myself from feeling?

I AM WHERE I AM—NOT WHERE
I THINK I SHOULD BE.

You may feel rushed or in a hurry to get to the next phase of your life. This is actually preventing you from getting there. Whether you are trying to lose weight, meet a soul mate, or get clarity around your life purpose, when you focus on being there, you miss being here. When you can fully accept where you are, you will get where you want to go much faster. Be present. It will give you what you want.

◇ ◇ ◇ ◇

I am connected to my loving light and am present in this moment. I let go of all forced actions and stop trying so hard to get there. Instead, I accept fully where I am today. I am okay with this moment and accept my place in my life.

◇ ◇ ◇ ◇

What current situation in my life have I been resisting?

Day 59

I WAIT FOR THE RIGHT TIME.

Your life is unfolding perfectly, as planned. Fate and freewill are balanced, and you are living it in this moment. If you want something but are unsure of the next right action, consider that the Universe will guide you when the time is right.

If it feels forced to move forward, it is. It is not yet time. You will get clarity in the pause. Take time to review your plan and allow the Universe to show you the right time.

◇ ◇ ◇ ◇

I align with my heart, and I trust the Universe's plan. All things unfold in their right time and place. I am living my truth by being powerful in the pause. I only take action when I feel pulled from my heart. I wait for the right time and when it feels right. I will consider a steadier pace and wait for my heart's guidance.

◇ ◇ ◇ ◇

Where in my life do I feel forced to take action?

Day 60

I SURRENDER ALL EXPECTATIONS.

Expectations can cause negative thoughts. When you expect a great outcome and instead see a mediocre resolution, you may feel disappointed. This letdown may leave you feeling as though your dreams or desires are pointless. In this way, expectations can be damaging to your personal growth. By drawing this card, the Universe is telling you that you are putting too many expectations on an outcome. This may not be intentional, but chances are your expectations are holding you back. Perhaps when you care about something, you put your whole heart into it. There is nothing wrong with being passionate, but be careful not to put too much energetic stress on the specific outcome.

When you focus too much on how things will play out, you do not trust divine resolution. Trying to force a specific outcome to match your expectations can lead to frustrating results. Instead of manipulating and straining your energy, surrender your expectations by trusting all is in the right order.

◇ ◇ ◇ ◇

I am connected to my true self and know that all is in perfect order. I have goals and deep desires, but they will be manifested in their own right time and place. I release my need to have things when and how I want, and I turn my trust to the Universe. I always get what I need, when I need it. I surrender.

◇ ◇ ◇ ◇

Where have I been focusing too much on the outcome?

"

I Surrender
All Expectations.

"

Day 61

I OPEN MYSELF UP TO TRANSFORMATIONAL LOVE.

My dear, beautiful soul, you have so much love to give to this world. Your heart has been hurt, and you have closed it off from others. You've been trying to protect yourself and control your pain, but true love is waiting for you. True love is available to you when you love yourself first. Open yourself up to more love in your life by starting with love for yourself. Care for yourself in nurturing ways. Be kind and compassionate with yourself as you move toward your next phase of your life. Everything is unfolding in your favor as you open yourself up to transformational love. You deserve the love of your life, and it is coming sooner than you think, but first, give yourself the love you so desire.

◇ ◇ ◇ ◇

I am ready to receive love. I show up more fully by being present in my life. I take steps daily to cultivate more love in my life, starting first with loving myself. I have been hurt in the past, but my heart doesn't need to carry those burdens. I forgive my past and allow myself to open up to new potential. Love is available to me when I love myself first.

◇ ◇ ◇ ◇

How can I celebrate the love within myself?

I HAVE UNIQUE GIFTS AND TALENTS THAT THE WORLD NEEDS.

You are far too hard on yourself. There is a great talent and gift within you that the world needs, and only you can bring them forth. Stop focusing on others and instead turn your attention back to yourself. Focus on all of the experiences that have helped shape you and made you who you are. You have a special something that no one else in the entire world has. Let this truth motivate you and inspire you to action.

◇ ◇ ◇ ◇

Everything I have been through has helped prepare me for who I am becoming. My unique perspective, skills, talents, and story are a valuable part of my life. I have gifts that the world needs, and the more honest I am about who I am and what I want, the easier it is to express my authentic self. I show up for myself by expressing my true self and sharing my ideas with others and the world. I know that when I give the world my true self, the world will reflect and love my trueness back.

◇ ◇ ◇ ◇

What gift or talent do I have that I want to share
with others and the world?

Day 63

GRATITUDE IS THE LIFE FORCE OF EVERYTHING.

We can often look outside of ourselves and see someone else who looks happier, more satisfied, more successful, or healthier. When we focus on them, we can forget to be thankful for what's going well in our own lives. Turning your attention to gratitude instead of jealousy or frustration can help you see all of the blessings in your life. You may be focusing too much on what you don't have and what is not working. By turning your focus to gratitude, you will open up new opportunities. Thankfulness is the life force for all you truly desire. Your path will become less strained when you turn your energy to love and gratitude.

◇ ◇ ◇ ◇

I am thankful for all I am and all I have. My life is a perfect reflection of all I desire and things I want flow to me naturally. My life is in perfect balance as I turn my attention to what I appreciate most.

◇ ◇ ◇ ◇

In what area of my life can I be more thankful?

Day 64

I HAVE THE COURAGE TO BE IMPERFECT.

You are perfect as you are. Your need to gain approval from others stems from an inner drive to be seen and noticed for who you really are. When you show up courageously as your true self, you will get all you truly long for. The imperfections you hide out of fear of judgment are actually qualities others will adore. Give yourself permission to be the real you.

◇ ◇ ◇ ◇

I am perfect in my imperfections. They help me be realer and more relatable. I embrace all aspects of myself, including the areas of my character I try to hide. I know that when I show my true self, I will be loved and respected. I have the courage to be the real me.

◇ ◇ ◇ ◇

What flaw that I hide from others can I reveal?

Day 65

THE WORST IS BEHIND ME.

Continue to forge ahead. You are coming into a time of your own, and the worst is now behind you. You have made great strides to overcome adversity and challenges. You can rest assured all your hard work will pay off. Now you will be rewarded.

◇ ◇ ◇ ◇

I am strong and powerful. I have worked hard to get to where I am today. The worst is now behind me, and I can celebrate my efforts. I gracefully move forward with confidence as all of my right actions are now rewarded.

◇ ◇ ◇ ◇

Where can I celebrate a job well done?

I GRACEFULLY ACCEPT ALL CHANGES HAPPENING IN MY LIFE.

You may feel like certain situations are out of your control and life is happening at you rather than for you. Today is a gentle reminder that everything you experience is always for your highest good. If you are in a situation that feels uneasy, simply turn your attention to what is going well in your life and you will be more graceful in the transition. You are entering into a new phase of your life; with this newness sometimes comes uncertainty and stress, but when you align with your desires and what you truly want, you will see that all the changes you are currently experiencing are part of your bigger life plan. Everything is always in the right order.

◇ ◇ ◇ ◇

I accept what is and take a proactive approach to my life and goals. Each day I show up fully by choosing love and kindness. As I move forward into the unknown, I accept what is and gracefully step forward into the life unfolding in front of me. All is in the right order, now and forever.

◇ ◇ ◇ ◇

What change has been stressing me out?
How can I relax more into the transition?

I AM VIBRANT AND IN PICTURE-PERFECT HEALTH.

A healthy lifestyle starts with a healthy mindset. Feeling vibrant from the inside out will help you feel more balanced in all areas of your life. When you focus your energy on good vibes, you will feel connected to your true self. You are always healthy and vibrant when you shine your light. Instead of focusing on the trouble areas of your body or diet, use this time to cultivate new habits that help you feel healthy.

◇ ◇ ◇ ◇

I am healthy and connected to my body. I care about what I put in my body, and I make conscious choices to aid in my healthy energy. I choose foods that make me feel alive and healthy. I am healed from all sickness and disease. My body is a beacon of true energy and pure light. I am love. I am healthy.

◇ ◇ ◇ ◇

What healthier habits can I start?

Day 68

IT ISN'T WHAT I HAVE THAT MATTERS. IT IS WHAT I DO WITH WHAT I HAVE.

You might be focusing too much on what you don't have. But remember you have everything you need inside of you to get to where you want to go. You have been given a unique set of gifts and talents that only you can bring forward. Stop spending so much time on what you don't have and start to embrace and use what you do.

◇ ◇ ◇ ◇

I am connected to my true self. I have a unique power in me that can help me with everything I need in life. I spend my time honoring my unique self and use my talents wisely. I understand it is not how the cards fall that matters but how I proceed forward with what I have been dealt.

◇ ◇ ◇ ◇

What can I do even with my current limitations?

Day 69

MY DREAMS WILL ONLY SUCCEED WHEN I TAKE A CHANCE ON THEM.

Your dreams are important, and they come to you for a reason. When you are inspired, you should take action. Look at a recent dream of yours that manifested into reality. It took courage and dedication, but you did it. Give yourself the recognition you deserve and find it in you to do this again. Your future self is counting on you to take a chance on your dreams. You won't regret it.

◇ ◇ ◇ ◇

I am attracted to my future as my dreams are in full focus. I am a success and living proof of all that is possible. I choose to follow my heart in every moment as I move forward with courage and determination. My dreams matter. I respect them by fearlessly moving forward.

◇ ◇ ◇ ◇

What dream have I ignored but keeps coming back to mind? What action step can I take to move this dream forward?

IT'S THIS OR SOMETHING BETTER.

You may be focusing too much on a specific outcome and manifesting a goal in a certain way. This manifestation has not revealed itself so that you could be angry, worried, or frustrated. Repeat the mantra "It's this or something better," as you remember that there is a reason in the grand scheme of things for what is or isn't happening. The Universe has heard your prayers and desires and is going to deliver what you want. Patience and trust is needed right now, but what you experience may not be exactly what you want. If you are experiencing letdowns, it could be because you are focusing too much on a specific outcome. Trust that the Universe will give you what you truly need and you are always being guided. Instead of looking at the situation as a loss, consider that you are being protected and prepared for something much better for you. Remember, rejection is protection, so you are not actually at a loss. Instead, turn all your energy into what you truly want to feel and align with that energy. What you desire will come to you in the right form at the right time.

◇ ◇ ◇ ◇

I am no longer determined to reach my goal using the method I thought best. I see multiple ways to get what I want, and I am open to the Universe guiding me to the right next action. I am connected to my big picture, and it is this or something better.

◇ ◇ ◇ ◇

What disappointment in my life led me to
something even better?

Day 71

I BELIEVE IN WHAT I CAN'T SEE.

Miracles are happening around you in every moment. Just because you can't always see the fruits of your labor does not mean your efforts are in vain. Turn your focus to what you believe in and focus forward with confidence.

Just because you can't always see a situation playing out in the way you hope does not mean it is time to give up. Keep focusing forward and believe in what you cannot yet see. It will soon manifest into your life, and all your energy will pay off.

◇ ◇ ◇ ◇

I stand behind my dreams and believe in them with all my heart. I may not see the outcome in my current reality, but I know it exists and is on its way to me. I visualize my success and see myself actively achieving my desires. I believe, and I will achieve.

◇ ◇ ◇ ◇

What can't I see that I believe in?

Day 72

FEAR OF THE UNKNOWN IS A BYPRODUCT OF SETTLING. I DON'T SETTLE.

If you spend a lot of your time focusing on fears associated with the unknown, now is the time to release them. Perhaps you are allowing yourself to settle. You deserve more in your life, and you can move away from this fear-based thought pattern by aligning with your true worth.

◇ ◇ ◇ ◇

I am connected to my future by moving gracefully through the unknown. I understand that every step of my journey leads me to a deeper understanding of my honest self. I release all worry connected to the unknown, for I am safe and I am being guided.

◇ ◇ ◇ ◇

Where have I been settling?
What action steps can I take to raise my standards?

Day 73

MY SOUL IS ROOTING FOR ME.

You may be putting too many hours into a specific situation. It is necessary to recalibrate, rebalance, and refocus your attention, possibly in a new direction. Your soul is rooting for you and will guide you to take the next right action. When you turn inward and ask your heart what it needs, your soul will guide you to what you truly want.

◇ ◇ ◇ ◇

I have worked hard to get to where I am, and for today, that is enough. I celebrate all of my hard work and know I am being guided. My soul is rooting for me. I can make it through this tough time. My troubles disappear as I align to my true heart's purpose. I am connected to my soul, and I know it is celebrating my successes.

◇ ◇ ◇ ◇

What right next action am I being guided to take?

I FEEL MY FEAR AND DO IT ANYWAY.

Your fear is speaking to you, and it is an indicator of what you need to do. When the fear is loud and debilitating, you can be certain it is trying to show you something. Instead of being paralyzed by your fear, look deep into it and see what it is trying to show you. When you step through the fear, you will see it was a guidance system leading you to your true self. Feel your fear and, instead of turning away, go through it.

◇ ◇ ◇ ◇

I feel my fear and move through it with graceful attention. I see that my fear can lead me into new awareness of my authentic self. When my fear gets loud, it is an indication of what is most important to me. By stepping though my fear, I am touched with love and purpose. I step courageously into the next chapter of my life.

◇ ◇ ◇ ◇

What is my fear trying to tell me?

Day 75

MY LONELINESS IS NOT AN INVITATION TO SETTLE.

You may feel lonely, but this does not mean you are alone. Your loneliness can be a teacher of greater understanding of yourself and your true needs. Turn your attention to what you desire, and you will cultivate a deep awareness within. Instead of focusing on what is not available to you, give yourself the love you desire. The love you seek will soon find you.

◇ ◇ ◇ ◇

I am never truly alone. I may feel lonely, but I allow myself to feel this emotion. When I feel it, it moves through me, and I can release it. My loneliness is not an invitation to settle. I demand respect, and I align my life to my values. The love I deserve is on its way to me, but I first must give it to myself.

◇ ◇ ◇ ◇

What relationships have I settled in?
What steps can I take to raise my worth?

I AM KIND TO MYSELF. I KNOW I AM DOING THE BEST I CAN.

Everything you have ever done has been from a need to have or give more love, and love is never wrong. Instead of allowing your inner critic to run the show, treat yourself with kindness and self-respect. You are doing a tremendous job, and for today, it is enough.

◇ ◇ ◇ ◇

I take loving action and move forward in life with self-compassion and kindness. My life is unfolding as it is supposed to, and nothing I have ever done or said is wrong. Every choice has led me to where I am today. I am doing the best I can, and that is enough.

◇ ◇ ◇ ◇

In what ways can I be kinder to myself?

DAILY ACTION CULTIVATES CONFIDENCE AND CLARITY.

Today is an important reminder that your current situation is a direct result of previous actions and thoughts. If you are unhappy or feel unsure about the next right action to take, it could be because you lack confidence and don't have clarity. Instead of feeling overwhelmed lack, take action and watch the clarity unfold. To get more confidence, we must do the thing that we fear. In taking action through uncertainty, we become more certain, and things can fall into place with more grace and ease.

◇ ◇ ◇ ◇

I am not afraid of my future. I align my energy with good feelings and focus on what I want. When I feel uncertain, I take consistent action instead of dwelling on the lack of clarity. When I take action, my true path is revealed.

◇ ◇ ◇ ◇

What fear is holding me back?
What action step can I take in the face of this fear?

Day 78

I CAN TRY AGAIN.

You may be in a situation that has not worked out the way you wanted. You can always try again. Perseverance is essential as you step forward into the next phase of your life. The past is not a failure but an opportunity for learning. As you examine what didn't work, you will get clarity about what does work. Keep going and try again.

◇ ◇ ◇ ◇

I am in integrity and connected to my truth. I know my past situation is part of my bigger picture. Nothing is wasted or out of place. I turn inward to observe all my experiences and study them with an objective eye. As I learn what doesn't work, I become clearer about what does. I can always try again.

◇ ◇ ◇ ◇

What have I given up on that still wants
to be pursued?

I DON'T NEED A REASON TO HELP OTHERS.

You might think it is important to help others because it makes you a good person. Although this is true, ask yourself if you help others because it seems like the right thing to do. When you help those in need because of outside influences, it hinders your ability to truly help. Instead of focusing on what others need from you, or what looks right to others, give for no external reason.

◇ ◇ ◇ ◇

I am full of energy and love. I extend this love to those in need. I don't need a reason to help others. A desire to give my time, money, or energy is present within me, and I help those who need me. I release my need to look good and give from an honest place. I don't need any reason to help other than it makes me feel good.

◇ ◇ ◇ ◇

What organization do I feel strongly about?
How can I help?

Day 80

I LOVE MY BODY BECAUSE OF WHAT IT HAS OVERCOME.

You may resist or reject a current body part or your entire body. Your body is a vehicle for love, and it is always giving you guidance. Trust your body because it has overcome great challenges. Learning to love yourself includes embracing your body as it is today. Love your flaws away and you will be free of self-inflicted pain.

◇ ◇ ◇ ◇

My body is a tool for transformation because it always guides me to the right path. I listen to my body and the wisdom within. I love every inch of my body and celebrate its strength and power. I am strong and beautiful, and I love me.

◇ ◇ ◇ ◇

How can I send light and love to every cell of my body?

Day 81

I AM COMPASSIONATE WITH MYSELF.
IT TAKES TIME TO HEAL.

Just as there are many different reasons to grieve, there are also many different ways to grieve. Though people may move through the same stages of grief, each person takes a different amount of time to reach each stage. Maybe you have recently experienced the death of a loved one or the end of a career or relationship, and you are finding it difficult to move on. Others may tell you that you need to get over the situation, but your true self knows it takes time to heal. Follow your true self. Trust that you know what is best for you even when those around you attempt to push you through the healing process. Be compassionate with yourself during any time of grieving. All situations must resolve in their own time. Allow the healing to happen of its own accord.

◇ ◇ ◇ ◇

I allow myself to heal. I give myself as much time as I need to move on from my past. I know my past has helped make me who I am today, and I celebrate each moment that has led to right now. I am kind to myself and give myself time to heal these open wounds. It is okay to be in the healing process. I will give it time.

◇ ◇ ◇ ◇

Where have I been forcing myself to heal faster
than feels right?

I STOP BLOWING MYSELF OFF.

Your needs are important. You may give so much of your time and energy to others that you feel exhausted at the end of the day. Your desires matter, and this is a reminder to make yourself a priority. When you show up for yourself, others will be more fulfilled too. You will find more balance when you stop blowing yourself off.

◇ ◇ ◇ ◇

I show up for myself. My needs are important, and it is necessary to listen to them in order to live a balanced life. When I put my needs first, I am showing self-respect and self-love to the world and myself. When I show up for me, I can be more valuable to others.

◇ ◇ ◇ ◇

What loving act can I do for myself?

Day 83

I DO NOT CHEAT ON MY FUTURE WITH MY PAST.

Your past decisions may have made you the person that you are today, but hanging on to the negative emotions or guilt from your past is damaging to your future. Great power comes from making peace with your past decisions, but in learning to leave the feelings of those decisions in the past, you will truly grow. You have been hanging out emotionally in your past. Perhaps your thoughts have been consumed with how a situation played out, and you feel as though you have made a mistake. Maybe you can't forgive someone from your past, and you spend your energy trying to get resolution from the situation. The longer you stay in the past, the harder it is to move into your future. Forgive your past and you will welcome new opportunities into your life.

◇ ◇ ◇ ◇

I am present in my life. I forgive my past so I can walk into my future. My future is waiting for me with open arms and enthusiasm. I welcome the new phase of my life and release my energetic hold on the past.

◇ ◇ ◇ ◇

How have I been cheating on my future by
thinking thoughts of my past?

Day 84

MY UNIQUENESS IS WHAT MAKES ME OUTSTANDING.

You are too down on yourself. Those flaws you hide are part of what makes you beautiful. You may be trying hard to fit in, but this is making you feel more like an outsider. You were not born to fit in. You are here to stand out. Stop giving so much attention to the things you find flawed or ugly and shine light onto the awesome you that is.

◇ ◇ ◇ ◇

I am a unique child of the Universe. All that I am I celebrate. My unique quirks are part of my beautiful being, and I release my need to change myself to try to fit in. I am perfect as I am. I like me.

◇ ◇ ◇ ◇

What "flaw" can I accept today?

Day 85

THINKING I DON'T HAVE A CHOICE IS A CHOICE.

You may think that you have no choice, but recognize that this thought pattern is a choice in itself. When you focus on the lack of options available to you, you feel more stressed and worried. This can prevent you from moving forward in life. Instead of focusing on what is not working and how trapped you feel, turn your attention to the options available around you. You always have a choice to see things in a new light.

◇ ◇ ◇ ◇

I am in charge of my own life and make choices from an empowered position. Everything in my life is a choice, and at any time I get to eliminate what no longer works for me. I am brave and honest as I remove myself from situations that cause me stress or distress. I always have a choice to feel good and make joy my priority.

◇ ◇ ◇ ◇

What situation do I feel stuck in, and how can
I see it from a new perspective?

I AM ACCOUNTABLE FOR MY OWN LIFE.

You may be blaming other people for your circumstances or situations. Instead of pointing the finger at others, turn it around to yourself. What role did you play in this situation? Now is the time to be responsible. This is not about self-inflicted blame or punishing yourself. It is about taking responsibility so you can move forward.

Consider that everything in your life (whether or not you like it) is made by design, by you. You get to choose what stays and goes. So if you are unhappy with an area of your life, you have the power to change it.

◇ ◇ ◇ ◇

I am responsible for everything in my current reality. This is empowering because I can choose to remove anything and everything that no longer works for me. I do not blame myself for anything, nor do I punish others. Instead, I take responsibility, so I can move forward with clarity and focus.

◇ ◇ ◇ ◇

What situation can I take responsibility for?

Day 87

I DON'T ROMANTICIZE THE PAST. I CHOOSE TO BE PRESENT.

You may be spending too much time focusing on the good aspects of the past. Although it is wonderful to see the positive sides of all situations, this could be clouding your judgment and view. When it comes to people or situations, there is what actually happens and what we perceived that happened.

If you are only focusing on the good and failing to see the reality of the situation, you could set yourself up for failure in the future. Take off your rose-colored glasses and see the situation for what it really is.

◇ ◇ ◇ ◇

I am connected to my true self in this moment. When I reflect back on previous situations, I can see all realities. Others' motives are revealed to me when I take a nonreactive approach to my life. I step out of my past and choose to be present.

◇ ◇ ◇ ◇

What past situation have I been romanticizing?
How has this hurt my ability to move forward?

I AM NOT WHAT PEOPLE SAY I AM.

You might focus too much on what other people think of you. When others make comments or share their opinions, this has nothing to do with you. Learning to love yourself starts with releasing the need for approval from others. Focus all your attention on accepting yourself and you will be free of this external burden. Happiness can never come to you from the outside.

◇ ◇ ◇ ◇

I am okay with where I am today. I am no longer disillusioned by others' beliefs or opinions about me. The only thing I focus on is approving of my own self. I align with my truth, which is love and light. I matter, and I know I make a difference.

◇ ◇ ◇ ◇

Where have I been worrying too much about what others think?

Day 89

I LEARN THE WAY ON THE WAY.

Your dreams or goals may feel stuck or in a static mode right now, but that may be because you are trying to accomplish them using the same methods that failed you in the past. If you have been working hard to try and achieve specific goals or solve troubling situations, you may be ready to give up. Today is a reminder to keep going but consider a new approach to solving old problems. When you step out of your comfort zone and try new things, you will see refreshing results.

◇ ◇ ◇ ◇

I am open to trying new things. I solve old problems in fresh, innovative ways. I connect with my true self to align with my greatest good. When I move forward with confidence, I am at ease.

◇ ◇ ◇ ◇

What can I try again but in a new way?

Day 90

I LET GO OF WHAT THE UNIVERSE IS ASKING ME TO RELEASE.

What are you holding on to? The Universe has been guiding you to let go of certain things, habits, or people in your life that no longer serve you. When you hold on to things past their expiration date, you are not being true to yourself. Go inward and listen to your heart. It will gently guide you into the next right action for releasing old ways of being.

◇ ◇ ◇ ◇

I am open to living my life in expansive ways. I do this by releasing all old patterns, situations, and people that no longer serve me. It is not mean or selfish to put myself first. It is an act of self-love. I see evidence of my love-filled actions when the Universe guides me to new awareness and direction.

◇ ◇ ◇ ◇

What has the Universe been asking me to release?

"

My Purpose
Is to Live More on
Purpose.

"

Day 91

MY PURPOSE IS TO LIVE MORE ON PURPOSE.

There is a lot of focus spent on trying to reveal your true life purpose and the thing you think will bring you ultimate ful-fillment. Today is a reminder that the goal of your life is not to find just one thing to bring you joy but to live each day with more joy. That is the true purpose of your life. Focus on the things you love to do, and do more of them. Instead of trying to seek out only one big thing, create a life you love by carving out moments of fulfillment. Recognize that we are always changing and growing, so your life purpose is not a thing you do but rather the way you live. The purpose of your live is to live more on purpose.

◇ ◇ ◇ ◇

I am present to the life that is unfolding in front of me. I know that there is great learning in the unknown. Instead of trying to focus so much on finding my life purpose, I choose to live each moment more on purpose.

◇ ◇ ◇ ◇

How can I be more purposeful with my intentions?

PLEASURE IS MY PRIORITY.

You have been working extremely hard to make certain situations manifest. Recognize that there is a time for work and a time for play and overworking yourself will result in frustration, anxiety, and even physical pain. Instead of trying so hard to make things happen, relax into the pleasure of life. Make pleasure your new priority and seek out only things, situations, people, and experiences that give you a sense of satisfaction through pleasure. It is not selfish or wrong to want to live a life of pleasure. Tapping into the things that bring you joy will give you a more balanced appreciation for life.

◇ ◇ ◇ ◇

I embrace life's luxuries and relax with more pleasure. I am in control of my life and take each situation in stride. When I focus on things that bring me immense pleasure, I succeed in all areas of my life. Pleasure is my new intention as I seek it out with deliberate focus. All is in the right order when pleasure is in play.

◇ ◇ ◇ ◇

Where have I been denying myself pleasure?

Day 93

MY PLAN B COULD BE BETTER THAN PLAN A.

Are you holding on to a situation that no longer works? Perhaps you have recently gone through a change or transition and you are struggling to see the relevance. Sometimes the Universe will push us on to a new plan that contradicts our original path. Trust the Universe is leading you to your true path and seek out guidance.

◇ ◇ ◇ ◇

I am connected to my life's ultimate plan. I trust the Universe and see the plan unfolding in front of me. I embrace new opportunities for growth, and I expand with love and light.

◇ ◇ ◇ ◇

What plan feels forced or like it no longer fits in my life?
Can I let it go?

I AM ENCHANTED WITH LIFE.
I SEE THE BEAUTY IN EVERYTHING.

Life is opening up all around you. Learning to see the beauty in the seemingly small situations will open up your heart and mind. Look deep into your life and look at beauty in everything. Even washing the dishes can be an act of enchantment as you smell the bubbles and feel the warm water against your skin. In each activity you do, can you be more present?

◇ ◇ ◇ ◇

I am enchanted with my life. I am in joy and see the good in every situation. I feel open and expansive as I embrace all of the world's beautiful creations.

◇ ◇ ◇ ◇

Where can I pause and let more life in?

Day 95

PART OF LOVING MYSELF IS LETTING OTHERS HELP ME.

My dear, you are working far too hard on trying to make things happen. Your exhaustion is because you are not allowing help to support you. You may feel like you must do it all on your own, and the situation may feel impossible, but this is a gentle reminder that you have abundant support all around you. Being able to receive is an important part of living a balanced life. Being able to ask for help is essential to your growth, so use this mantra as a universal sign that it is time to stop working so hard to make things happen on your own. When you ask for help, you support yourself with love and you can solve old problems in miraculous new ways.

◇ ◇ ◇ ◇

I am not afraid to ask for support. I know there are abundant resources available to me. I just need to ask for help. I don't have to work so hard to make things happen. I can allow support and let the Universe help me solve my problems. Letting others support me is the most loving thing I can do for myself.

◇ ◇ ◇ ◇

Who can I ask for support?

WHERE I LIVE FEELS LIKE A HOME.

Do you love where you live? Your home is your sanctuary and source of inspiration. If you live in an environment that strains your energy, consider adding more love. Now could be a good time to begin making arrangements to move into a place you like more. If it is not time for you to move, you can add more comfort into your home with candles, soft music, and things you love.

◇ ◇ ◇ ◇

My home is a reflection of my best self. I honor where I live and care for my place. I know my home is a sanctuary, which allows me to be my best self.

◇ ◇ ◇ ◇

What does my home say about me?

HOW I FEEL IS MORE IMPORTANT THAN HOW I LOOK.

You might be worrying too much about what others think of you. If you are feeling self-doubt, self-loathing or self-blame, you might be trying to fit into the outside world. When you return to your true self, you will be reminded the only thing that really matters is how you feel. Focus more on how your life feels versus how it looks.

◇ ◇ ◇ ◇

I feel good. I am connected to my best self, and I choose healthy actions. I focus on how my life feels instead of how it looks. Happiness comes through my feelings and attention to the details of my life.

◇ ◇ ◇ ◇

Where have I been more focused on how
I look rather than how I feel?

MY EMOTIONAL PAIN SHOWS ME WHAT NEEDS TO CHANGE.

Sadness, depression, and heartache are gentle reminders to probe deeper into your life. Look at what is not working and be open to living your life in new ways. You will see that, one day, it will all make sense.

◇ ◇ ◇ ◇

I am connected to my emotions, and I feel them fully. Any area of my life that feels painful is an opportunity for me to go inward. I reflect on my pain and see what needs to be changed.

◇ ◇ ◇ ◇

Where in my life is the most pain?
What is it trying to tell me?

NO ONE CAN MAKE ME FEEL "LESS THAN" WITHOUT MY PERMISSION.

You are worthy of your desires, but you have to believe in yourself first. If you are waiting for others to approve of you before you step forward, you may be doing yourself a disservice. Instead of giving your power away to others, align with your intentions, and you will feel worthy of your desires.

◇ ◇ ◇ ◇

I am worthy of my desires and connected to my best self. I let go of others' opinions, as they have no bearing on my overall choices in life. I feel powerful and aligned with my true self.

◇ ◇ ◇ ◇

Where have I been feeling unworthy?

Day 100

I APPRECIATE THE PERSON
I SEE IN THE MIRROR.

You are too hard on yourself, especially with your physical appearance. The person you see in the mirror is not someone to turn away from in disgust. That person you see is your best friend. That person knows your heart and your desires better than anyone else, so trust the person you see in the mirror. When you become friends with yourself, everything else falls into place.

◇ ◇ ◇ ◇

I am my own best friend. I love everything about me, and I appreciate who I see in the mirror. I matter in this world, and my physical appearance is part of my life plan. The things I used to resist about myself have become my greatest tools of understanding for accessing my true self.

◇ ◇ ◇ ◇

I will go to the mirror, look into my own eyes,
and repeat "I love you" five times.

Day 101

I SURRENDER THE STRUGGLE.

Your struggle in life is a direct reflection of how tightly you are holding on to outcomes. Are you trying to make thing happen or worrying about outcomes that aren't happening the way you envisioned? When you struggle through life, you tend to focus on what isn't working, and your struggles are snowballing into one another. Instead of focusing on the issues that keep arising, ask your struggles for guidance. Consider going into a quiet meditation and asking your struggles, "What lesson do you have for me?" You will stop struggling when you can let go of trying so hard to make things happen how and when you want them to. Surrender and you will feel freedom.

◇ ◇ ◇ ◇

I am not off track in my life; everything is better than I realize. I let go of trying to make things happen how and when I want them to happen. There is a better outcome awaiting me when I let go of trying to figure it out. Instead of trying so hard, I let the Universe support me and solve my problems with grace and ease. I surrender the struggle.

◇ ◇ ◇ ◇

What problem can I step away from and let
work itself out?

Day 102

I AM MAKING A BIGGER IMPACT THAN I REALIZE.

You've spent a lot of time seeking others' approval and trying to get people to appreciate you. This message comes to you because it is time to see your own worth. You are making an incredible difference in the lives of others even if it doesn't feel that way. Many people have been positively impacted by your actions and look to you for inspiration even if they never tell you. You are needed in this world and a gift to the people around you. Instead of feeling let down or unappreciated, turn your focus inward and appreciate yourself. Give yourself what you are seeking and you will soon see the impact you make in this world.

◇ ◇ ◇ ◇

I am here for a reason, and I make a difference by just being me. I am making a huge impact in the world by expressing my truth and being honest with myself as I shine more love. I care deeply about those around me, and this love and kindness is reflected outward in the world. I am making an impact by expressing my authentic truth.

◇ ◇ ◇ ◇

What act of kindness have I done recently?

I HAVE DETERMINATION AND WILLPOWER.

You may feel shattered by recent setbacks. But getting back on the horse is part of your overall plan. Persistence is important right now as you reach your goal. Today is confirmation you have what it takes to reach your potential. Take steps out of your comfort zone and try new routines. The bravery you show will reward you with confidence and joy.

◇ ◇ ◇ ◇

I am connected to my higher self. I am proud of how far I have come and see all my setbacks as miracles in disguise. I am determined and will reach my goals with effortless grace and ease. I am empowered and connected to my accomplishments. I take pride in how far I've come.

◇ ◇ ◇ ◇

Where can I allow myself to feel more pride in what
I have accomplished?

I HAVE A SUPPORT SYSTEM THAT WOULD DO ANYTHING FOR ME.

You are not alone. You have amazing people around you who can give you strength and courage. Others are available to help you when you allow the support into your life. The meaning that you are seeking will come through interactions with others and the support you receive.

◇ ◇ ◇ ◇

I am open to other people's guidance and support. The challenges in my life will be removed when I seek out help. I am being guided to the right mentors, friends, and relationships to assist me for my highest good.

◇ ◇ ◇ ◇

How can I get out of my comfort zone and ask a
new friend for support?

I DON'T WASTE TIME WITH NEGATIVE THOUGHTS.

Your thoughts affect your outcome. When you spend time thinking about what isn't working and focusing on the negative aspects of yourself and others, you prevent yourself from seeing opportunities that are available to you. Don't waste your precious time with negative thoughts. Life is too short. Flood yourself with white light and repeat kind thoughts to yourself. You are beautiful as you are; you don't need to change. The truth is, you don't have to believe everything you tell yourself. Be kind, starting with the way you talk about yourself to yourself.

◇ ◇ ◇ ◇

I refuse to participate in the drama of the world. I understand that loving intentions first start with me. I am kind and compassionate with myself, and I love myself with each positive thought. I speak kindly to myself, and I let compassion lead the way.

◇ ◇ ◇ ◇

What part of my life can use more positivity?

I EMBRACE MY EMOTIONS.

Your emotions are trying to tell you something. Listen to the wisdom within. When you feel sad, let yourself feel the emotions. It is okay to cry and be vulnerable. If you are happy, allow yourself to feel the happiness. You might be pushing your emotions aside in an effort to maintain the status quo. When you embrace your emotions, you will be free.

◇ ◇ ◇ ◇

I am fully present with my emotions. I allow myself to feel each feeling as it arises. When I feel my emotions, they help guide me to a deeper awareness of self-actualization. My emotions are a strong guidance system. I trust them.

◇ ◇ ◇ ◇

What emotion have I been hiding?
I allow myself to feel it.

I CELEBRATE OTHERS' SUCCESSES.

Do you feel jealous or concerned that others have something you want? When you focus your attention on how you lack what you want, you keep yourself from receiving it. Instead of condemning others for their successes and opportunities, celebrate them as if they were your own. The Universe is abundant and full of opportunity for all. You will get what you desire when you hold love and light for others.

◇ ◇ ◇ ◇

I am alive and full of life. I set myself up for success by celebrating all good things in life. When others are rewarded, I sing in praise and joy alongside them. I am connected to my life, and I celebrate others' wins as if they are my own. There is no place for jealousy in my life. I turn all my attention to what I want and use others' successes as a possibility for my own future.

◇ ◇ ◇ ◇

Who can I congratulate and celebrate for a recent success they have had?

I NURTURE MY INSTINCTS.

You have an internal guidance system guiding you in every moment of your life. Your instincts are your strongest force forward. Nurture them with love and give your gut feelings more priority in your life. Your instincts will never lead you astray.

◇ ◇ ◇ ◇

I listen to the internal voice that guides me forward. I have an awareness of self that allows me to confidently move forward in life with conviction and attention to detail. I nurture my instincts by trusting myself in each new situation.

◇ ◇ ◇ ◇

What are my instincts trying to tell me about a situation that has caused me angst?

I IMAGINE MYSELF LIVING
MY IDEAL LIFE.

You might be experiencing a situation that feels constricting or forced upon you. This is a reminder you are only trapped by your current focus on the situation.

From a spiritual standpoint, everything we experience is an illusion that we are separated from love. If you feel emotional pain or turmoil, you may be trapped in fear. To break free from this, look at the illusion of what is versus what could be. Send your energy and attention to feelings of self-love and then to feelings of love in general. Surround your "what could be" with love and you will glide through all troubling times.

◇ ◇ ◇ ◇

I am not a victim of my current situation. I focus my thoughts on loving energy and choose to see the truth during troubling times. I know I am capable of moving through difficulty, and I am only trapped by my negative thoughts. I turn to positive expectations, and I am free.

◇ ◇ ◇ ◇

What positive things could be in my life?

Day 110

MY CREATIVE PURSUITS ARE REWARDED.

Your ideas matter, and pursuing your creative side is important right now. You may feel uncreative or uninspired, but honoring your creative impulses will serve you well. Being creative is not about what you do or how it looks. It is about what you experience. Give yourself permission to be more creative and express your artistic side. You will be rewarded for expressing your free-flowing nature.

◇ ◇ ◇ ◇

I am open to showing my creative side. I have ideas worthy of pursuing. When I am inspired, I act, and my creative pursuits are always rewarded. When I am creative and honor my expressive nature, I am free and open to inspiration.

◇ ◇ ◇ ◇

What creative project can I start?

IT IS NOT FLOWING BECAUSE IT IS NOT THE RIGHT TIME.

Now is not the time to give up or surrender your goals but to simply recognize everything has a universal timing that manifests at the exact right moment and in the highest good for everyone involved. A feeling that the outcome is uncertain may cause you to doubt your desires, but you must not lose faith in your focus. Simply surrender your need to have it happen at a specific time. The Universe is working behind the scenes to make things happen for you exactly when they need to, and if they aren't happening yet, it doesn't mean they won't. Now is a time for patience and trust. Do not give up, but do not worry about when it will happen, because when it does happen, it will be at the best possible time for you within your entire life plan.

◇ ◇ ◇ ◇

I will not give up on my goal, but I will let go of when it needs to happen. I believe in divine timing and trust the process as my life plan unfolds. I know that everything happens at the right time and the right place for all involved. I surrender my need to have it all figured out, and I stop trying so hard to make things happen when I think they should. When they do happen, it will be better than I ever imagined.

◇ ◇ ◇ ◇

In what area of my life can I trust the timing more?

Day 112

I AM UNAPOLOGETIC ABOUT WHAT MAKES ME HAPPY.

You might be putting too much emphasis on other people's opinions of you and your actions. Return to your desires and get in touch with why you want them. When you connect with the why, this will move you forward with energetic ease. The more you do what makes you happy, the happier you will be. It won't matter what others think about you or your life because you will be living your authentic joy.

◇ ◇ ◇ ◇

I am connected to my joy. I do what makes me happy, and this in turn makes others happy. When I align with my honest desires, I am rewarded with love and support. I am unapologetic about who I am and what I love.

◇ ◇ ◇ ◇

Where can I be more unapologetic about what brings me joy?

Day 113

SELF-LOVE IS A PRACTICE I
SHOW UP FOR DAILY.

Self-love is not selfish, nor is it something that just happens. It is a practice that you show up for every day. Taking care of yourself is not just about what you eat or how you look—it is about how you talk to yourself about yourself. Lately, your inner critic may be in overdrive, telling you that you're aren't good enough or smart enough or attractive enough. Well, tell your inner fear voice, "Enough." Focus on being kind to yourself and practice self-love by becoming your own friend. When you show up for yourself each day, your life becomes more manageable because you are more grounded and balanced.

◇ ◇ ◇ ◇

I choose to be kinder, more loving, and more compassionate with myself. I show up for myself each day by taking positive action toward my goals and prioritizing self-care.

◇ ◇ ◇ ◇

How can I show up more for myself today?

I CELEBRATE THE MINI MIRACLES.

There are infinite miracles happening every moment all around us, but we are often too overwhelmed to see them. You may be focusing more on the struggles and what isn't working well. Today's mantra is a reminder to be mindful of the blessings that occur all the time. Turn your attention to what is thriving and celebrate the little victories. This will also help you relax and feel more balance in all areas of your life.

◇ ◇ ◇ ◇

I am grateful for the blessings in my life. There are many indications of my desires manifesting into form, and I love the mini miracles happening all the time. I focus my intentions on celebrating and seeing more miracles come to form.

◇ ◇ ◇ ◇

What mini miracle can I celebrate?

I AM COMFORTABLE IN THE SILENCE.

When was the last time you allowed yourself to sit in silence? Silence is an important activity to create balance in a happy life. Allow silence to guide your true focus forward. Instead of trying to control conversations or situations by filling them with words, consider a quieter approach. Being in silence can open up new clarity for your life. You will have a remarkable awareness of your true self when you allow silence to guide you forward.

◇ ◇ ◇ ◇

I am comfortable in silence. I do not need to fill my quiet time with words and noise. Instead of panic or constriction, I release my fears and I let love in. Silence is an opening to guidance I want to receive. When I am silent, I can hear my heart speak. I honor silence.

◇ ◇ ◇ ◇

Can I sit in silence for a few minutes each day?
(Give it a try now.)

I RETREAT INWARD FOR INSPIRATION.

You have motivation and strength inside of you. Turning inward will help inspire your life in all areas. Show more gentleness to yourself and see the connection to everything. Your inside world will reflect into your outer world. Any situation you find yourself in will require a more sensitive approach by retreating inward for ultimate inspiration.

◇ ◇ ◇ ◇

What I am is love. What I choose to manifest is more love. My true self inspires everything I do, which is a reflection of true love. I am full of love and kindness and compassion, and I express my real self to the world. In all my experiences, I choose to focus inward for answers.

◇ ◇ ◇ ◇

How can I allow more inspiration in my life?

WHEN I GIVE, I ALSO RECEIVE.

Perhaps you have been holding on too tightly to your finances. When you share resources with others, more abundance can come to you. You may feel like you don't have enough time or money to share with others, but this may mean you are holding on too tightly. When resources are not shared, it will close off and block the abundant energy from coming to you. Also pay attention to your energy and emotions. Are you giving enough of yourself to the world?

◇ ◇ ◇ ◇

I am happy to share my true self with others. I give my time and energy to those who are in need of support. My resources can help others, and I share my gifts openly and without expectations. When I give, I receive so much more in return.

◇ ◇ ◇ ◇

Where can I give more time, money, or resources?

EVERYTHING HAS AN EXPIRATION DATE.

There is an innate timing to everything in your life, including endings and departures. Everything in your life arrives at the exact right moment to help you grow and learn more about yourself and life. People, places, and even situations are all universal assignments designed to help us grow. Sometimes we hold on to things that no longer serve us, and when this happens, it prevents us from stepping into the next phases of our lives. Recognize that everything has an expiration date. This includes people, places, and things—even remaining in jobs or other environments could be holding you in the past. When you respect expiration dates and let things go, you are honoring the natural process of life, which means the things that are supposed to come to you can enter your experience much faster.

◇ ◇ ◇ ◇

I am not worried about the next phase of my life. There are certain things in my life that are asking to be released, and I let them go now. I trust the natural outcome and know that I am safe and secure through this transition. The things in my life that have expired have helped me become who I am, and for that I am thankful, but it is now time to let them go. I release them with ease.

◇ ◇ ◇ ◇

What expired situation in my life am I still holding on to?

WHAT I SEE IN LIFE
DEPENDS GREATLY ON WHAT
I'M LOOKING FOR.

What you see in your life is a reflection of your original focus. Whatever you dedicate attention to will manifest. If you are dissatisfied with results in your life, return to your thought patterns about the situation. If you want more joy-filled results, focus on more positive thoughts.

◇ ◇ ◇ ◇

I am aligned with my original intentions. All is in right order in my life because I am actively living the results of my actions and loving thoughts. I am connected to my truth. I am happy with the results in my life.

◇ ◇ ◇ ◇

What results am I dissatisfied with?
How can I reframe my focus?

Day 120

MY LIFE IS IN PERFECT BALANCE WHEN I LISTEN TO MY HEART.

The key to success in your life is balance. If you are feeling overwhelmed or stressed out, take a deep breath in and return inward to your heart. In order to create successful solutions, you need to align with what brings you joy in the moment. This is a balancing act you can master. When you make choices from a deliberate place of love, you are calmer and more peaceful and your life is in balance.

◇ ◇ ◇ ◇

I focus on my accomplishments, for I've done a great job. My life is in perfect balance because I take care of myself and follow my heart. I allow myself to be recognized, and I embrace the power of the pause. I take care of my needs and honor my inner desires. My life is in perfect balance when I listen to my heart.

◇ ◇ ◇ ◇

What is my heart telling me?

THINGS FALL APART BECAUSE BETTER THINGS ARE FALLING INTO PLACE.

You are holding on to parts of your life that are supposed to be released. It may feel like things are falling apart and you have no control over anything, but this is a universal realignment for your life. Instead of looking at your situation with fear, see the changes as an opportunity for your highest good. Everything that you are currently going through is part of your soul's growth. Naturally, you may want to resist, but this only holds off the inevitable: you are changing. Let yourself change with your life. Your future is bright, and there are good things in store for you.

$$\diamond \quad \diamond \quad \diamond \quad \diamond$$

I do not resist the changes unfolding in my life. I allow myself to step gracefully into my future as I let go of the past. There is nothing for me to do except release the burden of holding on to what is no longer working. I let go and let my life flow.

$$\diamond \quad \diamond \quad \diamond \quad \diamond$$

Where have I been holding myself back?

Day 122

I LET GO SO I CAN LET MYSELF GROW.

You are in a time of incredible growth and deep transformation. Things may feel difficult, and the struggle you feel can be painful, but this is because you are holding on to what is trying to be released. Let go and let yourself grow. Let go of what you cannot change and step into the unknown, and these unfamiliar places will start to feel more comfortable. Just like a caterpillar that is turning into a butterfly, you must not interrupt the flow of your own life. Imagine: If the caterpillar pushes through the cocoon right before it transforms into a butterfly, it will miss its true essence and life plan. Don't let fear hold you back! Let yourself grow by letting go.

◇ ◇ ◇ ◇

I am being asked to grow right now. I am transforming, and this phase of my life is supported by my highest good. I allow myself to flow naturally into the next chapter of my life. All is in right order when I let go of what no longer works so I can become who I am meant to be. I am safe and secure and trust the process.

◇ ◇ ◇ ◇

Where have I been holding myself back?

"

I Let Go
So I Can Let
Myself Grow.

"

THERE IS NOTHING TO FEAR.
LOVE IS HERE.

You have been trapped by fearful thoughts and illusions. You may feel overwhelmed by anxiety, and this is because you are focusing more on what is wrong with the world and your own life. Do not be in fear, for love is always close by. You have a universal energy and support system that is waiting patiently for you to ask for help. You also have people around you who would love to support you and remove the burden of fear you carry around. Allow yourself to open to the loving presence around you and within you.

◇ ◇ ◇ ◇

I release my fear and focus on the love around me and within me. I know that I always have a choice, to believe my fear or to align with love, and I choose to let love lead me. There is good in the world when I choose to see it.

◇ ◇ ◇ ◇

What fear can I see as false?

I GO BEFORE I KNOW.

You may feel unsure of which direction to go in your life. Perhaps you are at a crossroads or are unclear which route to take. Today is a gentle reminder that unless you take a step forward, the path will not reveal itself. When you take action, even before you know the right path, you will instantly see the right direction for you. Trust yourself and go before you know.

◇　◇　◇　◇

I am confident even when I do not know the best move forward. I take action by aligning myself with my internal light. When I connect to my inspiration, I can move forward with conviction and clarity. I go before I know.

◇　◇　◇　◇

What action step can I take despite my insecurity
or lack of confidence?

129

Day 125

NEW OPPORTUNITIES FOR HAPPINESS ARE ON THEIR WAY TO ME.

You can throw your hands in the air and declare, "It's over." Perhaps a situation has recently ended in your life and now is a time for celebration. You can look to your future and see opportunities coming your way. Happiness is a choice, and it starts with you turning your focus to the happy times instead of the bad.

◇ ◇ ◇ ◇

I see happiness all around me. I focus my energy on the good in my life, which removes the bad. I know new opportunities are part of my life's plan, and I am open to receiving more happiness and love.

◇ ◇ ◇ ◇

What happy times can I focus on?

I BREAK FREE FROM ALL THAT IS HOLDING ME BACK.

You are not your past, nor do you need to spend any more time focusing your energy on what has happened to you. Instead of dwelling on what could go wrong or what has gone wrong, see these as just fears from your past trying to replay in the present. You are bigger than anything that can ever happen to you, so turn inward and release the confines of fear. You are stronger than you will ever know.

◇ ◇ ◇ ◇

I am strong, determined, focused, and excited for my future. I refuse to let my past stop me from moving forward. I am a trailblazer, blazing a trail of happiness and hope wherever I go. I am free from my past. Nothing will ever stand in my way. Everything that I desire is possible and is on its way to me.

◇ ◇ ◇ ◇

What is standing in my way?
How can I release its hold on me?

Day 127

I COMMIT TO MY DESIRED OUTCOME.

It is important to keep going. Do not give up on your desired outcome. You are much closer than you realize, and giving up will cause you to regret in the future. This is your time. Celebrate how far you've come by envisioning the outcome exactly how you want it to be. Use the power of visualization to see your dreams through to reality. When you believe anything and everything is possible, it is, and soon enough you will be living your desires.

◇ ◇ ◇ ◇

I am focused and create my reality with deliberate intention. I focus on what I want and take guiding action daily. I am committed to my dream life, and this requires me to show up daily for myself and my desires. I am dedicated to the pursuit of my own excellence. I achieve all that I believe.

◇ ◇ ◇ ◇

What outcome can I focus more clearly on?

Day 128

THE FASTEST WAY TO IMPROVE MY SELF-CONFIDENCE IS TO DO THE THING I FEAR.

You may feel insecure and shy. But today is a reminder that the very thing you fear is what will bring you freedom. When you move through your fear and take loving action forward, your insecurities will fade. Confidence comes through taking action steps; your fear will disappear and be replaced with love when you do.

◇ ◇ ◇ ◇

I am fearless and free of worry. My self-confidence is flourishing as I step into my future with love and purpose. My fear is only an indication of what I care about, and I bust through all fears with action steps forward.

◇ ◇ ◇ ◇

How can I bust through my fear?

I PRAY FOR THE HIGHEST GOOD OF ALL INVOLVED.

The situation that is causing you the most stress can be solved. All you need is to turn your focus to your higher power and surrender your worry. Pray for the highest good for every single person involved. As you let go of your need to have the situation work out the way you think is best, you will see the Universe has a plan that is for your highest good. Know that you are being cared for and everything will work out the way it is supposed to.

◇ ◇ ◇ ◇

I release my need to have the situation resolved in a certain way. Instead, I surrender the entire process over to my higher power. I pray for the highest good for every single person involved. The situation will resolve itself when I stop worrying.

I let the Universe take the lead.

◇ ◇ ◇ ◇

What situation can I hand over to the Universe?

Day 130

I AM ONLY TRAPPED BY MY ILLUSION.

You might be experiencing a situation that feels constricting or forced upon you. Today is a reminder you are only trapped by your current focus on the situation. From a spiritual standpoint, everything we experience is an illusion of separation from love. If you feel emotional pain or turmoil, you may be trapped in fear. To break free from this, look at the illusion of what is versus what could be. Surround your "what could be" with love and you will glide through all troubling times.

◇ ◇ ◇ ◇

I am not a victim of my current situation. I focus my thoughts on loving energy and choose to see the truth in all troubling situations. I know I am capable of moving through difficult times, and I am only trapped by my negative thoughts. I spend time focusing on what I want instead of what I don't want. I turn to positive expectations, and I am free.

◇ ◇ ◇ ◇

What *could* be in my life?

I FIND A WAY TO KEEP GOING.

Your motivation may be dwindling. Remind yourself why you started and keep focus on the big picture. You will benefit from making mini goals within your big plan. Setting smaller attainable goals will help you stay on track. If the situation you are losing motivation with feels forced, do not push it. You will be better off taking a more playful, relaxed approach than powering through it. Take a break, go for a walk, take a bath, or enjoy a tasty treat. You will return to your situation with refreshed eyes and determination.

◇ ◇ ◇ ◇

I am focused and free from the fear of failure. I am worthy of my goals, and they are coming true for me. My motivation comes from inspiration in my heart. I align with my truth, which keeps me on track. I add more childlike wonder to my projects, and I feel happy and free.

◇ ◇ ◇ ◇

What am I trying to power through?
Can I consider a more fun-loving approach?

Day 132

WHO I BECOME IN THE PROCESS OF REACHING MY GOALS IS MORE IMPORTANT THAN ACHIEVING THEM.

You are putting far too much attention on the outcome. Your goals are important, but you are missing the grand learning right in front of you. The journey is the beautiful reward for you because you are becoming more of who you really want to be. Instead of focusing so much attention on the outcome, recognize that what you are learning is essential for you to be able to receive what you desire. The process is just as, if not more, important than your goals because you get to grow into your dreams.

◇ ◇ ◇ ◇

I am willing to relax into a more natural flow of my life. I release my obsession with trying to get there and instead can see the beauty in where I am now. I see that I am growing and becoming more of who I need to be to receive the goal I really want. I appreciate the process and am comfortable in the journey.

◇ ◇ ◇ ◇

How can I appreciate the journey?

IT IS REFRESHING TO GIVE LIFE TO OLD PROJECTS.

You have really good ideas. You should give yourself more credit for the projects you started in the past. Instead of feeling like a failure, look at the projects as opportunities for growth. Through each venture, you have learned more about what you want and don't want out of your life. Perhaps you want to return to a project. Get back into the joy of the process of creating and enjoy the journey.

◇ ◇ ◇ ◇

I am full of creative energy and lighthearted fun. My inspiration flows. I return to old projects with new life. It is refreshing to revisit old projects as they help me explore my creative side. My ideas are powerful, and they want to manifest into full form.

◇ ◇ ◇ ◇

What project can I give new life to?

IT ISN'T WHO I AM THAT HOLDS ME BACK. IT'S WHO I THINK I AM NOT.

You are spending too much time focusing on what you can't do. Instead of spreading the negative energy, focus your thoughts on what you are capable of. You have a life force inside you far greater than you could ever imagine. Put your attention on your talents, strengths, and good qualities. This will help you feel more secure and confident.

◇ ◇ ◇ ◇

I have talents and strengths unique to my life purpose. I celebrate my strengths and show them openly with love. When I connect to my heart, I am guided by my intuition and I am connected to my real self. I focus on who I am rather than allowing my fears to dictate my identity.

◇ ◇ ◇ ◇

What part of myself is holding on to fear?
How can I let it go?

THINGS MOVE FAST WHEN THEY ARE RIGHT.

When things are in the right order, they move at an effortless pace forward. If there is an area of your life that feels strained or forced, this is a reminder to stop pushing. You will find freedom in the flow. When you are on the right path, things will flow quickly and with great momentum. Enjoy the ride and trust you are being led in the right direction for your big picture.

◇ ◇ ◇ ◇

I am in a constant state of flow. My life unfolds effortlessly, and I am along for the ride. There is nothing I have to force, for all my plans are falling naturally into place. When things are aligned with my highest good, they happen rapidly. I am being divinely guided, and I trust this inspiration that comes to me. I take motivated action forward. My life is unfolding in the right order.

◇ ◇ ◇ ◇

What situation in my life has great momentum
and forward movement?

COMMUNICATION CAN SAVE ANY SITUATION.

An area of you life is not flowing as well as it could because of dishonesty or a lack of communication. The first situation that comes to your mind is most likely the situation to address. You may have a relationship that needs more focused attention; you can start by being honest with yourself and the other person involved. Communication can save any situation and help you feel more balanced. Ask yourself if you are being honest and speaking your mind. If you feel like you need to say something, now is the time to share your truth and speak up.

◇ ◇ ◇ ◇

I speak up and say what I need to say. I know that communication is needed in this situation, and I am open and honest with my true feelings. I speak with integrity and love. It is safe to address this situation openly and communicate my needs and desires.

◇ ◇ ◇ ◇

What do I need to say that I haven't yet?

I HAVE LOVING ALLOWANCE FOR OTHERS TO BE WHO THEY ARE INSTEAD OF WHO I THINK THEY NEED TO BE.

The situation you are in has already come to an end. From a big-picture sense, your life is unfolding according to plan. When you retreat inward, you can see the purpose in your pain. Every situation you have experienced has groomed you for the next chapter of your life. Instead of dwelling on the sadness, focus on the silver lining and the light at the end of the tunnel.

◇ ◇ ◇ ◇

I am okay. My life may not be perfect, but it is perfect in this moment. I allow myself to feel every part of my journey, which means I am present and aware. I see the light inside of me as it reflects out into the world. When I follow the light, the darkness disappears.

◇ ◇ ◇ ◇

What is the silver lining of my current situation?

I LOVE ME.

You are amazing, beautiful, magnificent, and perfect just the way you are. Millions of people can tell you this, but if you don't believe it yourself, none of the outward love will resonate. Today is a gentle reminder to see yourself the way people who love you do. Your life will be so much easier when you can see how amazing you really are. Self-love is not selfish but rather a beautiful act of kindness. The world needs less criticism, blame, and hate. Start with yourself. Start today.

◇ ◇ ◇ ◇

I am beautiful. I am love. I am light. I love me. It makes sense, because to love myself is to have less hate in the world. I choose to be my own friend.

◇ ◇ ◇ ◇

What loving act of kindness can I do for myself today?

I KNOW WHEN TO MOVE ON.

You don't need to stay in any situation that has expired. You might be holding on to a relationship that is supposed to end. When we progress on a personal development path, our friends or loved ones don't always come along. If you have someone in your life bringing you down, consider this a sign that it is time to move on.

◇ ◇ ◇ ◇

I know when to move on. I don't hold on to anything that is supposed to be set free. I listen to my inner voice, which tells me when it is time to seek out new friendships and release the old. I energetically cut the tie between negative friends and family. I connect to my own love and light.

◇ ◇ ◇ ◇

What relationship can I remove myself from?

THERE ARE INFINITE RESOURCES AVAILABLE TO ME.

When you have been stuck doing the same thing for so long, it may seem as though there are no other options available to you. You might feel a lack of resources or feel that you can only focus on your limitations. However, when you give yourself time to think about your problem, you will find there are an infinite number of solutions for you. Instead of spending your energy looking at what you do not have, turn your attention to the multiple solutions available. You just have to be willing to see new opportunities. There are infinite resources available to you. Trust that you will be guided to the right one.

◇ ◇ ◇ ◇

I am guided to release all limitations and negative beliefs. I turn my attention inward to seek my truth. I align with my heart's desires, which will show me the next right action. I step lovingly into my future with open arms as I embrace all the resources available to me. I am only limited by my thoughts. I release all limitations with love.

◇ ◇ ◇ ◇

What resources can I use to help me solve
a troubling problem?

MY ANXIETY IS NOT BASED ON REALITY.

When you have anxiety, you begin to feel as though it is you against the raging world. Everything may collapse on you at any moment, and there will be no escape and no one to help you. The entrapment you feel is not real. It is inspired by fear. The anxiety in your life is often based on false beliefs and fear-based thoughts. Disconnecting from these thoughts is difficult but necessary in order to gain mental clarity. Turn your fears over to the Universe and trust that you will receive the tranquility you desire. What you crave is inner peace and you will get that as you continue to show up for yourself and seek out guidance through mentors, new friendships, and connections with yourself.

◇ ◇ ◇ ◇

My anxiety is not real; it is inspired by fear. I release my limitations to the Universe. The clarity I seek comes from my connection with self. The more I am in tune with my body and heart, the easier my life will be. I let go of my worry and replace it with love.

◇ ◇ ◇ ◇

What anxiety can I release?

Day 142

I AM TENACIOUS WITH MY GOALS.
THEY ARE ACTUALIZED WITH LOVE.

Focus on your dreams with energy and passion. When you put love into the equation, your dreams manifest faster. Be tenacious and unapologetic about your desires. Your goals are part of your life plan. When you follow through on the inspiration that comes to your heart, you are living your purpose.

◇ ◇ ◇ ◇

I am in love with my life, and my dreams are coming true. I shine light on all areas of my life so I can remove the shadows and negative thoughts that once limited me. When I focus on my goals with passion and love, I will not fail. The Universe is supporting me in my life plan, as my ultimate wishes come true every day.

◇ ◇ ◇ ◇

What goal can I add more love to?

Day 143

I CAN ONLY TAKE RESPONSIBILITY FOR ME.

You have a big heart and care deeply for others. But you can't save others from the lessons they need to learn. You are only responsible for yourself. When you take care of other people's problems and fix troubling situations for them, they may not learn the lessons they are supposed to learn. You can help people by loving them and supporting them in the means that feel good for you, but at the end of the day, you are only responsible for yourself. You can't save or fix others—you can only love them.

◇ ◇ ◇ ◇

I do not enable others or allow them to walk all over me. I care deeply about the people in my life, but I have boundaries and clear standards. When others are hurting or need my support, I show up fully because I have already taken responsibly for me. I am healthy and happy and take full accountability for myself; therefore, I can be there for others.

◇ ◇ ◇ ◇

Where can I set a stronger boundary?

I AM WELL.

The wellness you seek is already inside of you. You may be feeling rundown or focused on disease. When you focus your attention on the disharmony in your body, you bring more attention to what is not working. Instead, focus on sending love and light to every one of your cells and picture your body healed.

◇ ◇ ◇ ◇

I am well. I am harmony, and I am light. I send loving energy to every cell in my body. I replace all disharmony with comfort and ease. I send love to my areas of pain and focus on healing and resolution. I am at ease with my body and my life.

◇ ◇ ◇ ◇

What thoughts of disharmony can I heal with
loving thoughts?

I AM CALM IN THE CHAOS.

There may be situations around you that you cannot control. Perhaps it feels like the walls are caving in. You may not be able to control those around you, but you can always control your own internal state. When you align with your own heart center, nothing will affect your true balance.

◇ ◇ ◇ ◇

I align to my heart's center and seek out the truth in all situations. What once bothered me no longer affects me, for I am peace and harmony. I can be calm in the chaos because I am a beacon of love and light.

◇ ◇ ◇ ◇

Where can I release my need to control my environment
and allow things to be?

I REPLACE JUDGMENT WITH CURIOSITY.

You may be trying to solve a problem by thinking your way through it. Perhaps your motivation has eluded you and the project has come to a standstill. Instead of forcing analytic thoughts into the equation, reflect your attention out into the world. Go explore life and watch your productivity increase.

◇ ◇ ◇ ◇

I am connected to all of life and see it as a balance and flow. I am inspired by my own experience and the life force energy around me. Everything I experience and everyone I meet is an opportunity to learn more about life and myself. I replace all judgment with curiosity.

◇ ◇ ◇ ◇

What inspires me?

I AM ONLY TRAPPED BY MY OWN ILLUSIONS.

The anxiety you feel is caused by your fear and worry. You may feel like you don't have a choice, but thinking this is preventing you from seeing the opportunities all around you. There is always a solution of the highest good, and the situation will unfold beautifully when you can see you are no longer trapped but actually surrounded by love.

◇ ◇ ◇ ◇

I am surrounded by support and see opportunities all around me. I am not trapped, as my fear is only an illusion. Only love is real, and I let love be my compass.

◇ ◇ ◇ ◇

What fear has been keeping me stuck?

Day 148

I KNOW IT IS NOT ABOUT ME.

You might be over analyzing and over thinking a situation. When events unfold and other people are involved, it is easy to fall into victim mode and wonder why they did or didn't do what you thought they would. Today's focus is on the inner knowing that you don't have to take things personally. What others do is a reflection of their own beliefs, fears, and thought patterns. Not everything is about you. Release your attachments to others. Now is also a good time to look at where you have been selfish in your life. Consider that it isn't always about you. Reaching out to apologize to someone might be helpful for you to move on.

◇ ◇ ◇ ◇

I disengage with the drama around me, and I know that what others do is not about me. I also look at my life and look at where I can add more love and self-compassion. I may have unknowingly hurt another person. It is my intention to make things right.

◇ ◇ ◇ ◇

Who can you apologize to?

I PASSED THE TEST.

You did it. It's time for celebration. You have recently experienced a challenging event or situation, and you overcame the challenge. Life is full of lessons and opportunities for growth. You will continue to repeat patterns until you learn the lessons you need to learn from them. If there is a situation you recently found yourself in, where you acted with new awareness, you have arrived at a new level of understanding. You passed the test and can celebrate your victory.

◇ ◇ ◇ ◇

I am the creator of my life, and I show up fully. I dive into each situation with awareness, compassion, and honesty. I remove unnecessary patterns in my life by being present and asking what I can learn.

◇ ◇ ◇ ◇

What patterns keep repeating in my life?
What can I learn from them?

I DETACH FROM THE DRAMA AROUND ME.

Situations, drama, and life events will always be unfolding around you. You have a choice to play into the drama or remove yourself from it. Your life will be productive, and you will feel more peace when you detach from the drama. Your dreams will manifest faster, and you will feel the peace you seek.

◇　◇　◇　◇

I remove myself from unnecessary drama and chaos. Everything I need is inside of me, and I focus inward for survival. The less I allow the outside world in, the safer, more secure, and more peaceful I am.

◇　◇　◇　◇

What drama can I disengage with?

I EXPLORE ALL MY OPTIONS.

Do not apply tunnel vision just to move through a given situation. Perhaps you have been too narrow-minded in your approach. Maybe you feel trapped and can see no way out. Take a step back and look at all angles of the situation. You have multiple resources available to you and many ways to solve this particular dilemma. Instead of focusing on the path of most resistance, expand your search beyond. Be open to receiving guidance and support.

◇ ◇ ◇ ◇

I am open to receiving guidance and support. I explore multiple angles and options, as there are infinite solutions available me. I trust everything is working out in my favor, and I move forward with effortless confidence and trust.

◇ ◇ ◇ ◇

Where have I been too narrow-minded?

Day 152

I'VE DONE NOTHING WRONG.

You put too much blame on yourself. You have done nothing wrong, yet you feel like it is your fault. The situations in your life are all part of a growing understanding that will transport you to your greater good. Instead of thinking things didn't work out, start celebrating how things have fallen into place. When you can shift your focus on what is wonderful instead of what is lacking, you will feel more connected to your true self. Forgive yourself and know that you did the best you could with what you knew at the time.

◇ ◇ ◇ ◇

I forgive myself for all my past mistakes. I see now that nothing was out of order and wrong. My mistakes are actually an opportunity for deeper awareness within myself. I cultivate self-love and inner peace through my situations and retreat inward for guidance. I know I have not done anything wrong. It is not my fault. I release self-blame and focus on love. I invite light in.

◇ ◇ ◇ ◇

What can I forgive myself for?

"

My Heart
Never Lies.

"

MY HEART NEVER LIES.

Your heart has a message for you, and it is time to listen. Deep within you is inspiration that wants to be manifested into the world. The dreams that come to you are not illusions but true insights into a happier, healthier, and more fulfilled you. Let yourself dream more and trust the inspiration within. Your heart is your truth.

◇ ◇ ◇ ◇

I am aligned with my truth. I know that the inspiration that comes to me is the truth, and it will make me happy when I pursue it with pleasure. My heart never lies, for it is love, and love is the only thing that is real.

◇ ◇ ◇ ◇

What is my heart telling me?

THE FASTEST WAY TO SOLVE THE PROBLEM IS TO STOP PARTICIPATING IN THE PROBLEM.

There are situations in your life that may not make a lot of sense. The problems are amplified when you participate in them and allow them to take over your mind. When you focus on the problems, talk about them, and think about them obsessively, it is impossible to come to a resolution. Instead of focusing your attention on the problem, be thankful for the clarity to see through the situations. If you don't have clarity yet and you have no idea how to make it through, pray for clarity. Ask for a sign. When you can ask the Universe for guidance, you will get what you need much faster, as the support can rush in to help.

◇ ◇ ◇ ◇

All problems in my life are pathways. I see them as opportunities to grow and learn. Instead of focusing on the problem, I let myself relax into the truth, which is that problems go away when we stop focusing on them. I release my need to try to fix the situation and allow the solution of the highest good to reveal itself. All is in the right order.

◇ ◇ ◇ ◇

What problem can I stop obsessing about?

I DON'T SECOND-GUESS MYSELF.

Stop second-guessing yourself. Everything you've ever gone through has prepared you for this. You can do it. Believe in yourself. The only thing stopping you is fear based on insecurity and worry. But you are more ready than you give yourself credit for.

◇ ◇ ◇ ◇

I am ready for this. I can do this, and I am confident in my skills and talents. I know that the ideas that come to me are part of my life's plan, so I act with courage and grace as I move forward.

◇ ◇ ◇ ◇

What am I worried about?
How can I move forward and stop second-guessing myself?

I TAKE TIME TO REST.

Your body needs time to heal. You have been working extremely hard and pushing to make new things fall into place. Instead of working so hard, retreat inward and seek the celebration in the pause. Taking time to rest will help cultivate a deeper awareness of productivity and focus. You may feel like you are missing out and that is why you are working so hard. But when you can slow down and relax, you give what you want a chance to come to you. If you feel unproductive and cannot relax, use today to experience relaxation. Can you go for a nature walk, sit in silence, and let meditation become a practice? Will you take a nice bath or read a new book? Taking time to rest is an act of self-love. When you rest, you show the Universe you trust the divine order of everything.

◇ ◇ ◇ ◇

I am productive and successful. All of my goals are being met because I balance my time well. I encourage relaxation and seek out ways to care for myself. I listen to my heart and let my body tell me what it needs. The wisdom in my body is the key to my success. I understand the power in the pause and return to the present moment when I relax.

◇ ◇ ◇ ◇

How can I relax today?

Day 157

I AM FLOODED WITH GRATITUDE.

There is infinite energy and support around you at all times. When you feel down and out, immediately turn your attention to the love and support around you and within your soul. When you look, you will see how abundant, successful, pretty, and happy you already are. Look on your life with gratitude and allow this energy to flood through all interactions. Being grateful will help you cultivate more abundance and love. Gratitude is the life force of everything.

◇ ◇ ◇ ◇

I give thanks to all that is in my life. I do not focus on any negativity or drama, but instead hold space for opportunities and expansive growth. I know everything is working out for my greatest good. I trust divine timing and celebrate all the good in my life. I am grateful for everything.

◇ ◇ ◇ ◇

What am I most thankful for today?

Day 158

I TURN MY ANXIETY INTO EXCITEMENT.

You feel uncertain right now, and this is a natural part of life. But when we stay stuck in our anxiety, it is because we are overthinking the future and potential outcomes we don't want. Your anxiety may be related to uncertainty and frustration about a situation that has not resolved itself. Anxiety is a form of fear manifested into feeling, but you have the power to turn your anxiety into excitement. Instead of letting the fear consume you, focus on the opportunities that await. You always have a choice: you can focus on what you don't want or what you do. Setting your eyes on what you truly want will bring more excitement to you, and this process will naturally reduce anxiety.

◇ ◇ ◇ ◇

I am at peace, and all is well. I trust myself and am comfortable with my life's natural unfolding. I do not put pressure on myself to figure out the future; instead, I trust the right outcome will happen at the right time. My life plans are unfolding perfectly, and I am excited about the outcome.

◇ ◇ ◇ ◇

What anxiety has been holding me back?
How can I turn the worry into trust and excitement?

I SEE LOVE EVERYWHERE.

Believe in miracles and the power of good. When you look for evidence of love, you will see it everywhere. Miracles are manifestations of love and support. Allow yourself to witness and be present for all that is great.

◇ ◇ ◇ ◇

I believe in miracles. I see them everywhere I look. I know I am a miracle, and when I shine my light, I help others. I trust the Universe is working with me to release all worry and fear. I am being led with intention and loving energy. I am a miracle.

◇ ◇ ◇ ◇

What miracle have I recently witnessed?

THE BEST ADVICE IS FELT IN MY HEART, NOT DIRECTED FROM MY HEAD.

Stop trying so hard to figure out what will happen. You are working overtime to try to come to a resolution. It is important to go after what you want, but when you try to control every situation or manipulate the outcome, you are not trusting the universe or the higher plan it has for you. Chances are your ego, the fearful voice in your head, has been pushing you to work harder and override any inspiration trying to come through from your heart. When you can get out of your own way and let your ego stop running the show, you will soon hear the whisper of guidance from your heart. Your heart's wisdom has the capacity to solve the problem in effortless ways, so let your heart lead you and trust the advice that is felt within.

◇ ◇ ◇ ◇

I release my need to control any situation, and I let my fear subside. I no longer work so hard on making things happen. Instead, I let my heart lead the way. My heart has a message for me, and it is my divine mission to listen to it daily.

◇ ◇ ◇ ◇

What is my heart telling me to do?

Day 161

EVERYTHING HAPPENS FOR A REASON.

The art of surrender is a process guided by love and light. If you grasp onto outcomes, people, or situations in fear of losing what you have, you restrict the flow of positivity into your life. Friendships grow close and then drift apart. A season of success in your career flourishes and then comes to an end. You may have to pack up and move to a whole new place where you don't know anyone. Recognize that your life has different chapters, and each of these chapters has beginnings and endings. Just like plants flower in the spring, are green and lush through the summer, and then go dormant in fall and wintertime, so too do our lives pass through different seasons that are necessary for our continued growth. Know that nothing is ever lost. The memory will stay in your heart forever.

◇ ◇ ◇ ◇

My life revolves around gratitude, no matter my changing circumstances. I embrace all situations that come to me and release situations, people, and ideals that no longer belong in my life. Every season in life is part of a greater cycle, and I honor that with an accepting heart.

◇ ◇ ◇ ◇

How can my releasing one part of my life
lead to new growth?

I SEEK OUT SANCTUARY.

A lot of information is coming at you at every moment of the day. It is wise for you to seek out time to retreat inward and find sanctuary. Take time each week to show up for yourself by removing yourself from technological distractions and current events. Treat yourself to life's simple luxuries and feel your soul become uplifted in joy.

◇ ◇ ◇ ◇

I allow my soul to rejuvenate by treating it to the simple pleasures of life. I rest in the moment and seek out sanctuary for my spirit. When I unplug and pause, I rediscover a new sense of self, one full of peace and joy.

◇ ◇ ◇ ◇

What sanctuary can I seek?

THINGS AREN'T ALWAYS WHAT THEY SEEM.

There is an element to your situation that is not fully in focus. You may be trying to move forward, but the situation feels stalled. This is because everything is not always as it seems. Situations, places, and people: the first thing that comes to your mind is the situation you want to address. You may be holding back and afraid to express your truth, and when you hide a part of you, you don't give others a chance to see the real you. This creates a false illusion and barrier between you and the rest of the world. Other people do this as well. You may be feeling uncertain in a particular situation, and this is because you are empathically feeling the disharmony in those around you. Send love to the people closest to you and speak your own truth. You will soon see others open up, and the barrier will be removed with love.

◇ ◇ ◇ ◇

I am a beacon of love and light, and I have important things to say. My values matter, and I stand up tall, empowered to be me. I understand that situations may feel uncertain and things aren't always what they seem. Instead of judging or turning to worry, I look for the truth in everything.

◇ ◇ ◇ ◇

What situation in my life can use more
understanding and care?

I ATTRACT WHAT I WANT BY BEING WHAT I DESIRE.

You, my dear, are working so incredibly hard to make your desires happen. Part of manifesting is learning how to let go and receive what it is you truly desire. You can attract what you want by becoming that essence yourself. For example, if you want to meet your soul mate, focus on loving yourself unconditionally. The love, care, and attention you give yourself will draw to you more of what you want.

◇ ◇ ◇ ◇

Instead of trying so hard to make what I want happen, I relax into knowing and trusting that what I want wants me too. I can manifest my desires faster when I give myself what I am looking for. I love myself for all that I am and all that I am becoming.

◇ ◇ ◇ ◇

How can I give myself what I want most?

LIFE IS A BALANCING ACT OF HOLDING ON AND LETTING GO.

There will always be situations in your life that are difficult to accept. Loss of people, paths, and possessions can throw us into highly anxious states and can consume our minds with negativity. Now is the time to remember that everything that happens to you moves you toward the path of your best self. Sometimes people, places, and situations must be let go in order for you to continue to thrive. Letting go is a loving, light-filled process. Grasping onto the things in your life that are familiar limits the light that can enter your life through openness to change. Letting go of the familiar also means letting go of fear and allows positivity to flow into your life.

◇ ◇ ◇ ◇

I am grateful for everything in my life. I embrace all of life's situations and often release situations, people, and ideals. Life is a balancing act of holding on and letting go, and I have mastered this.

◇ ◇ ◇ ◇

What am I holding on to that wants to be released?

CHANGE IS THE CATALYST TO HARMONY.

It's happening all around you: change. You can't avoid it, as it is the one guarantee and constant in life. Change is always in process, and when you resist it, you keep yourself in a place of stunted growth. Instead of holding on to the comforts of what is, recognize that change is growth. Change is an opportunity for you to transform and grow more into who and what you want. The transformation is where harmony and balance can happen. Chances are there are things in your life that aren't working as well as they used to. These situations, people, or circumstances once helped you grow into the person you are today, but as all things in life have an expiration date, so do these. It is time to release the hold and let yourself grow. You have outgrown them, and balance will ensue when you relax into the change instead of holding on to what is no longer working.

◇ ◇ ◇ ◇

I trust the process and recognize that change is a constant I can count on. All change is happening for me and giving me ample opportunity to grow. I look forward to the new experiences, places, and lessons as I transform into who I am really meant to be.

◇ ◇ ◇ ◇

What change am I looking forward to?

I PUT DOWN THE PITY PARTY.

Release the need to be right and stop blaming others for your own situation. Today is an empowering opportunity for you to take responsibility for your life. You are living a creative adventure, and the more present you are, the happier you will be. Instead of being the victim of the harassment of your life, stand tall and move forward with conviction and understanding. You are only as weak as you allow yourself to be. Rather than focusing on what happened and how you may have been wronged, focus on what you learned. Your power lies in how you pick yourself up and move forward.

◇ ◇ ◇ ◇

I have no shame or worry. I release all fear. I take full responsibility for my life and the role I played in each situation. I stand tall, confidently embracing this next phase of my life. I make powerful choices aligned with my true self. When I retreat inward, I am reminded nothing is out of order or place. Everything that happened helped me learn more about myself. I send love and light to others, including myself.

◇ ◇ ◇ ◇

Who am I blaming for my misfortune?
I send them love and forgive them.

I AM THE HERO OF MY OWN LIFE STORY.

You have been through so much in your life, but you have a choice. You can look at mistakes from your past with regret and throw emotional hate onto others, or you can overcome all of these challenges with love. Everything you have ever experienced is part of a bigger picture. You have a unique story that is yours to share. You will empower others when you share your real self with them. Just like the hero who has overcome life difficulties, you too will rise above the pain to show your true purpose. You are the hero of you own life. Start showing up as the hero and the overcomer.

◇ ◇ ◇ ◇

I am the hero of my life's epic journey. I have overcome great difficulties and survived the challenges. I am heroic in my nature and accept my power into grace. I stand tall with courage and a dedication to self for the greater good. When I show up for myself, I help others. It is my mission to help and make a difference. I can do this by being true to myself.

◇ ◇ ◇ ◇

What epic challenge have I overcome?

I AM UNAPOLOGETIC ABOUT MY NEEDS AND DESIRES.

Do not apologize for being who you are and wanting what you want. Other people may not get what you are doing or fully understand your mission, but it is not for them. It is for you. Your life plan will unfold more gracefully when you allow yourself to be who you really are and let go of worrying about others' opinions about you. You will soon find your life will flow with more joy when you are unapologetic about who you are and what you need.

◇ ◇ ◇ ◇

I release all worry tied to expressing my true self. I let go of thinking I need to look, act, or be a certain way, and instead I express my true self with courage and joy. I have desires that are essential to my own well-being, and I am open and honest with myself and others about who I really am.

◇ ◇ ◇ ◇

What desire can I be more courageous about pursuing?

WHEN TWO OR MORE PEOPLE ARE GATHERED, MIRACLES HAPPEN.

Spiritual scripture and gurus say that when there are two or more people gathered together in prayer and intention, miracles can happen. Today is about community and reaching out to loved ones for support. You have something within yourself that is important, and the world needs your light and love. When you come together with another person and share your true self, intentions, and desires, you can get the added benefit of more universal support. The power of two is a magnetic number for creation. You will have more energy focused on what it is you truly desire, and this can manifest stronger outcomes. Don't be afraid to get involved in your community.

◇ ◇ ◇ ◇

I am not afraid to stand up and shine my light. I come together with others to support the causes, ideas, and beliefs that are important to me. I do not resist but instead love. The love within me is the light the world needs. I share it openly and with compassion. I come together with loved ones and share my desires, needs, and hopes. I allow myself to feel supported and cared for, because there is infinite support and love around me when I open myself up to it.

◇ ◇ ◇ ◇

Who can I reach out to, to support a desire of mine?

I LOVE MY LIFE.

You may be spending a lot of energy focusing on what is not working. This is a natural human tendency. But for today, celebrate all that is well. No matter where you are in your journey to happiness, you have a wonderful life. When you focus on the amazing accomplishments, personal triumphs, and beautiful friends around you, you will see how loved and abundant you are. Celebrate your awesome life and focus on the positive aspects.

◇ ◇ ◇ ◇

I am in love with my life. I smile brightly as I beam with love. Everything in my life is perfect as is. I release all worry and pain because I know I am cared for and loved. My life is as beautiful as I am.

◇ ◇ ◇ ◇

What do I love about my life?

I'M NOT INFLUENCED BY WHAT WAS.

What was in the past has no bearing on what will be. Life is always unfolding into the next phase. The past is part of the present, but you get to create a new future. Most of us fear change and the unknown because we think what has happened in the past will happen again. But the law of attraction and energetic shifts in the Universe help to create a new reality if you truly want it. Instead of focusing on what you don't want, focus your energy on what you do want. Keep an optimistic mind about the creation of your desires. When you let go of what was and focus fully on what you truly want, there is always positive momentum that will assist you in manifesting the outcome you truly desire.

◇ ◇ ◇ ◇

What has happened is not an indicator of what will happen. This is a universal law: positive intentions create positive results, so if I want a different outcome than what I have experienced in the past, I focus forward with confidence, clarity, and daily action. The more I focus and visualize what I want, the easier it will be to get what I truly desire. I release my attachment to the past and let go fully of any and all karmic ties. I am free to be me as I step into my future.

◇ ◇ ◇ ◇

What future do I want for myself and loved ones?

WHEN I AM FEELING ANGST, I ASK, "WHAT IS THIS SITUATION TRYING TO TEACH ME?"

Every situation in your life is an opportunity to learn more about yourself. Instead of resisting or looking at the pain as frustration, turn inward and ask what you can learn here. The lessons available to you will help you move through the situation with more grace.

◇ ◇ ◇ ◇

Every situation I am in is an opportunity to learn. I grow into my true self by diving into the lessons. I remove fear as I step forward with confidence and purpose. I retreat to my heart and allow my inner voice to show me the truth of all situations. I am open to learning.

◇ ◇ ◇ ◇

What can I learn from this pain?

MY POSITIVE THOUGHTS CREATE DESIRED RESULTS.

You have an opportunity to create a more fulfilling outcome than what you are currently experiencing. If you are unhappy with an area of your life and you worry things are not going as well as you hoped, your thoughts could be the cause. Check in with yourself and see if your thoughts about the situation have been more negative than positive. There is no room for negative thoughts in the manifestation process. Allow yourself to go inward and reach for thoughts that make you feel good. Positive thoughts will help you manifest your desires more rapidly. We get what we focus on, and you have the power to get what you want by focusing on the positive aspects.

◇ ◇ ◇ ◇

I no longer focus on what is going wrong and instead turn all my attention to the outcome I desire. I know that remaining positive is essential for me to manifest my ideal outcome. I focus fully on what I want and release all fear and negativity by focusing on positive thoughts.

◇ ◇ ◇ ◇

What result am I currently unhappy with?
How can I be more positive about the situation?

I ACKNOWLEDGE MY DISCOMFORTS.

Your body has a message for you. When you are in pain or discomfort, it is not something to ignore or resist. Instead of looking at the discomfort as painful, look at it as purpose. There is purpose to all discomfort in your body. When you go inward and ask why you are hurting, your inner knowing will reveal the truth. All discomfort in your body and life is an opportunity to look at what is not working.

◇ ◇ ◇ ◇

I acknowledge my discomforts by sending each one love and light. I release the pain and trust it will be removed from my life. The pain I feel is part of my past, and I no longer resonate with it. I can learn from all body aches and discomforts. As I seek the truth, I am revealed the opportunity for expansion.

◇ ◇ ◇ ◇

What discomfort can I embrace?

I REFUSE TO PARTICIPATE IN THE DRAMA OF THE WORLD.

You don't have to participate in the drama around you. You may be looking for an exit from all the fear, and what you seek is in your own heart. Believe in your own potential and detach from negativity. Turn off your television, unsubscribe from newsfeeds, and regain your sense of balance as you put more trust in divine order. You always have a choice: you can dive into the drama or you can detach. Choosing to look for the good through the bad will give you strength and endurance so you can overcome any and all difficult life challenges.

◇ ◇ ◇ ◇

I detach from the negativity, drama, and pain in the world. I protect myself by taking care of me and choosing love. There is drama but only if I participate in it; instead, I choose to focus on love and light, and I know I am safe and secure when I align with my higher power's love.

◇ ◇ ◇ ◇

What negative situation can I detach from?

TIME IS ON MY SIDE.

You may feel pressed for time, and deadlines may be in your face, but time can expand for you. When you add more joy into what you do, you will have unlimited time and potential. If you are stressed out because you are trying to meet a deadline, consider a more playful way through the process. If you are powering through it, you may be missing the point. Adding more playful energy will help you be more productive as well. The more fun you have, the more successful you will be.

◇ ◇ ◇ ◇

Time is nothing but an illusion. There is no time, only space. I stand powerfully in this moment, accepting all that I am. I have endless amounts of time in front of me, and I meet all my demands. I add more joy into everything I do, and time expands.

◇ ◇ ◇ ◇

When do I lose myself in the moment and forget about time?

I DON'T HAVE TO MOVE ON TO LET GO.

You may be feeling at a loss with a recent event or the closing down of a relationship, situation, or dream. The Universe might be nudging you to move on and let go, but you're feeling conflicted. If you are navigating a broken heart, you can retreat into your heart for guidance. Your heart will lead you to let go, but this is different than moving on. You can emotionally forgive and release relationships, situations, or dreams by letting go of the outcome. When it is time to move on, you will know. You don't have to rush or force anything.

◇ ◇ ◇ ◇

I am okay with where I am today, as I know I am right where I need to be. I don't force anything in my life, including relationships, situations, or dreams. I balance the art of letting go with moving on. I trust I don't have to move on, but I can emotionally release the energetic hold of each troubling situation.

◇ ◇ ◇ ◇

What have I been trying to let go of
but can't move on from?

IT'S OKAY TO CHANGE MY MIND.

Part of your frustration could be because you are holding on to a situation that no longer serves you. It was a great choice for you at the time you made it, for it has helped you become who you are today. But you have learned what you needed to become who you really want to be. It is okay to change your mind. The insights that have been coming to you are part of your greater life plan. Trust them, honor them, listen to them. Do not feel guilty or worry about changing your mind, for in the transition you will see the freedom the new choice will give you.

◇ ◇ ◇ ◇

It is okay for me to let go of the current situation that no longer brings me joy. I can step gracefully into my future when I honor the inspiration that has been coming to me. I seek the freedom that comes from letting go of a choice that no longer serves me. I know that it is okay to change my mind.

◇ ◇ ◇ ◇

What decision no longer feels expansive and joyful?

I DON'T TAKE ANYTHING PERSONALLY—IT'S NOT ABOUT ME.

What others say and do have nothing to do with you. It is a reflection of them and their own points of view. Others' opinions shouldn't affect you. Do not let what they say about you distract you from seeing how amazing you are. Others may do and say things that don't feel good to you, but you don't have to buy into their belief systems. Instead of giving your power away, focus on your strength and the amazing things you offer this world. You are special just as you are; let your beautiful, natural self glow.

◇ ◇ ◇ ◇

I am not worried about others' opinions of me because I am aligned with my truth. I do not take anything personally because I am beautiful as I am. What others say and do are more about them than me, and I am okay with holding space for others to project their truth out into the world. I don't take their behavior on myself, nor do I let it distract me from being real and honest with myself. I let myself be who I am instead of who others think I need to be.

◇ ◇ ◇ ◇

What situation can you forgive that has caused you frustration or emotional harm?

I AM THE KINDEST PERSON I KNOW.

Kindness is the best way for you to navigate through any difficult situation involving another person. Being kind will help you seek the truth of all matters. When others offend you or stab you with words, you don't need to take on their harmful intentions. Simply connect back to yourself and align with your inner light. You can forgive them and send them kindness and love.

◇ ◇ ◇ ◇

I am kind. I choose not to associate with fear-based thoughts or attacks from other people. Instead of judging others for their actions, I hold my internal strength by aligning with kindness and peace. All is well in the world when I show my true self—the kind, loving, and peaceful person I know I am.

◇ ◇ ◇ ◇

What act of kindness can I do right now?

I SEE THE WORLD AS A BEAUTIFUL, KIND, AND LOVING PLACE.

It is a universal law that we always get what we focus on. If you are overwhelmed by life situations, it could be because you are paying extra close attention to the world events and news. The media captures and projects situations and amplifies them, which can cause more fear, mistrust, and worry. But for every bad situation that is broadcasted and highlighted, there are millions of mini miracles happening all around the planet. Look for the good and see the light in the world; kindness is all around us, but it starts with you. Be more compassionate with yourself and others, share yourself openly with more love, and you will soon see the world as a beautiful, kind, and loving place.

◇ ◇ ◇ ◇

I am protected, I am safe, and I am secure. I focus on the joy in this world and see kindness everywhere. It is not naïve to turn away from the hate and pain—it is self-loving to protect myself from harm. I can do this by seeing and sending more love to everyone everywhere. Healing the world from pain can start with me.

◇ ◇ ◇ ◇

To which part of the world can I send more love,
light and prayers?

I CAN FIND COMFORT IN MY PAIN.

You pain is not trying to distract you from life but give you guidance on how to heal and grow. The pain is not putting you off track but rather giving you clues into your soul's life lessons that are important for your own personal growth. Your pain is not something to run from but simply go into with a greater awareness of healing in the process. The pain you feel is a pathway to an awakening ready to be realized.

◇ ◇ ◇ ◇

There is comfort in my pain as I heal and grow. I see this not as a setback but as an opportunity to become more of who I really need to be. I am healing. I am growing. I am safe, and I am secure. I feel my feelings and let the pain move through me. As I sit presently with the pain, it is released from my life, and I am free to move forward.

◇ ◇ ◇ ◇

What pain can I sit with instead of running
away from?

I WAS BORN TO DO THIS.
IT'S GO TIME.

When you are confronted with an opportunity to reach your goal, you may still find ways to stall yourself from accomplishing it. This may be a self-sabotaging habit, but it most likely is a form of fear. Maybe you are afraid that when you reach the goal it will not be what you expected or that you will not have the success you thought you would. Stop procrastinating and go for it. You are capable of reaching your desired outcome and more equipped than you realize. You have everything you need inside of you. You just need to take forward action. Use all of your energy and insight to move the situation or project into full focus. It is go time, and you are in a place to accomplish great things. Believe in yourself and you will succeed. You were born to do this.

◇ ◇ ◇ ◇

I am motivated and inspired to move forward with my creative ideas. I am connected to my purpose, which means the momentum is working with me to achieve my desired outcome. I work swiftly and focus on my dreams with clear action and insight.

◇ ◇ ◇ ◇

What opportunities are within my reach today?

"

I Was Born
to Do This.
It's Go Time.

"

Day 185

REAL LOVE IS UNCONDITIONAL
AND NEVER ENDS.

You don't have to be so hard on yourself. The relationship that ended will forever be part of you because it lives in your heart. When others tell you to move on, you may feel burdened with pressure. But your soul knows there is nothing to move on from. Real love never dies. It will always live in your heart. The situation and experience may change form, but you will forever and always be connected in your hearts.

◇ ◇ ◇ ◇

I am connected to my heart. Real love never fades—it just changes form. I embrace the journey of life as some love changes shape, but it never changes in my heart. Love is love, and that is all there is.

◇ ◇ ◇ ◇

What person have I been forcing myself to get over?
Let love lead the way.

WHEN I CHERISH MYSELF, I SPEND MY TIME WISELY.

Your life is precious, and so are you. When you actively focus on self-care and cherishing yourself, you will gravitate toward situations, people, and things that uplift your life experience. Spending quality time doing things you love with people you care about will become your natural way of living. Cherish yourself and appreciate yourself for all that you have been, all that you are, and all that you are becoming. When you appreciate yourself, you will find you spend your time more wisely. All of a sudden, time expands, and you have enough time to do what you love.

◇ ◇ ◇ ◇

My life is precious, and so am I. I choose to do things I love, and I focus on bringing more joy to each situation in my life. When I appreciate myself, my time expands, and I no longer stress about not having the resources or time to do what I want. I cherish myself, for I am a beautiful being and I have a lot to offer this world.

◇ ◇ ◇ ◇

How can I cherish and appreciate myself more?

Day 187

I AM MORE ON TRACK THAN I GIVE MYSELF CREDIT FOR.

We all have moments when we feel like we aren't moving ahead. You may feel trapped by circumstances—like your efforts aren't leading to the hoped-for results. You might begin to feel like you're on the wrong track or like you're not enough. But those uncomfortable feelings are sometimes an indicator that you're growing in ways beyond your wildest beliefs. All growth requires change, and the changes you find yourself in are indicators that you are more on track than you realize. Celebrate where you are instead of where you think you need to be.

◇ ◇ ◇ ◇

I am more on track than I realize, and I am doing a great job. I celebrate how far I have come. I release all shame and guilt tied to my situation and see the good in where I am. All is in the right order.

◇ ◇ ◇ ◇

What recent accomplishment
can I celebrate and honor?

I HAVE THE COURAGE TO BECOME
WHO I AM MEANT TO BE.

It isn't who you are that is holding you back. It might be who you think you aren't. Instead of listening to your fears and insecurities, focus on who you really are. Honor your strengths and share your talents with the world. Have courage to be true to yourself. It is the greatest gift of all.

◇ ◇ ◇ ◇

I am courageous with my life. I show the world who I really am with confidence. I like who I have become, and every day I am becoming more of who I am supposed to be. I honor myself by showing the world my true colors. I am courageous with my life. I am becoming who I am meant to be.

◇ ◇ ◇ ◇

Where can I be more courageous with my heart?

JUST BECAUSE IT HASN'T BEEN DONE DOESN'T MEAN IT CAN'T BE.

Society puts a lot of pressure on you to be and do things differently than you want. You may have a goal or dream inside your heart, but it has never been done before. There is no need to abandon your dream. The fact that it has never been done gives you leeway to create the path forward. Because it hasn't been done before means you get to write the rulebook. If you are honest with yourself, you will seek your truth. And you have dreams that yearn to manifest. Despite the conditions of the world, go for it.

◇ ◇ ◇ ◇

I can do it. I am able to achieve greatness. The world is my playground, and I joyfully leap through all obstacles. I am a force of energy and focus. When I put my mind to something I desire, it will come true. My head and heart are aligned, and I courageously carve out new territory for my dreams to come true.

◇ ◇ ◇ ◇

What have I always wanted to do that has
never been done?

IT'S ALL FOR ME.

Imagine that everything in your life is orchestrated by design for you. Every person you meet is a character in your story; every challenge in your life is meant to help you grow. When we adopt the mindset that life is happening for us rather than to us, we can relax into its rhythm rather than trying to fight it. Think about what that means: Everything you are going through, have gone through, and will go through are parts of a bigger plan. It is all for you.

◇ ◇ ◇ ◇

It is all happening the way it is supposed to be because I am growing and learning more about myself through my experiences. I no longer blame others for my situation and instead take full responsibility for my life as a grand, creative endeavor. I see now that everything happens for me, not to me.

◇ ◇ ◇ ◇

What current challenge is helping
me grow the most?

Day 191

I TAKE RESPONSIBILITY FOR MY HAPPINESS.

You are doing a phenomenal job at life. No one gave you a manual on how to live a happy life. You have to seek it and carve out joy for yourself. You already know no one can make you happy but yourself. And you are showing up for yourself by reading books, taking courses, and following your heart's guidance. Happiness is a moment-by-moment experience; it's not just a destination but a way of life. Happiness is a mindset you cultivate the moment you choose to be happy.

◇ ◇ ◇ ◇

I am happy. I make a choice to be positive and see the good in my life. My happiness is not outside of me. It is inside of me, and I connect with it daily. I am in joy, and I am full of love.

◇ ◇ ◇ ◇

How can I take more responsibility for my joy?

THE GRASS IS GREENEST
WHERE I STAND.

Looking outside of yourself for happiness is preventing you from feeling the pure joy in this moment. When you seek happiness in places, things, people, or experiences, they may elude you. The grass is not greener over there. You may see evidence of this in your life as you explore new situations, hoping they will make you happy, only to find yourself stuck and sad. This happens because people try to fix problems by escaping them, but the problem will always persist until you water the grass where you stand. Focus on solving your current problems before running away from them.

◇ ◇ ◇ ◇

I am present in my life, and that means I water the grass I stand on. I know that no matter where I go, there I am, which means my problems, solutions and grievances will never disappear until I address them directly. I choose to compassionately solve all situations in my life, and I move effortlessly through transitions.

◇ ◇ ◇ ◇

What problem can I focus on fixing?

I DON'T WAIT IN VAIN.

If you are waiting for an answer or you want more clarity, focus all your attention on what you want. Don't give any energy to what you don't want. Your thoughts create your outcome. Hold faith. If you let your fears take over your thoughts, you will feel emotional pain. You don't have to wait in vain for an answer. Instead of being at the mercy of what others can give you, send love to the situation and ask the Universe, your guides, or higher power for support. Trust the situation will work out in your favor.

◇ ◇ ◇ ◇

Everything is unfolding perfectly, and I get what I want. The Universe is helping me become more of who I really am by giving me what I really need in life. I ask for what I want, and I wait patiently with love to receive my desires. When I am confident of the outcome, I wait without worry.

◇ ◇ ◇ ◇

What situation am I waiting on?
How can I add more life into the situation?

I DON'T KEEP SCORE.

Refrain from trying to one-up those around you. When you try to keep score, you damage your own potential for reaching your desires. By focusing on what others are or are not doing, you take attention off of yourself and your life's plan. Focus your attention back on your own desires and let go of trying to keep score.

◇ ◇ ◇ ◇

I do not judge others' actions or keep track of their mistakes. I am aligned with this moment in my life, and I stay present for all situations. It is not a race, nor do I need to try to one-up another person. I am aligned with my own self, which means I have nothing to keep score of.

◇ ◇ ◇ ◇

What scorecard can I erase?

MONEY WILL ALWAYS FLOW. MY SOURCE OF ABUNDANCE IS DIVINE.

If you are worried about finances, recognize where your fear is coming from. Do you have a lack mentality or believe there isn't enough? Some of the fears you carry might come from your parents. When we can look at our lack mentality and fears around scarcity, we can reverse them by focusing on the truth. The Universe is abundant and plentiful, so turn your attention on the opportunities instead of lack.

◇ ◇ ◇ ◇

I am always provided for because the Universe has an infinite amount of resources. There is plenty to go around. I release all my concern around lack of money and support. I am cared for, and I always have what I need.

◇ ◇ ◇ ◇

Where has scarcity or lack-based thought prevented me from doing what I love?

I AM EXTRAORDINARY.

You are not giving yourself enough credit. You are far too hard on yourself. If you could see yourself the way others do, you would be amazed. That little blemish, odd body part, or quirky characteristic is part of what makes you special. Start beating the drum of how fabulous you are and let go of insecurity and all self-blame.

◇ ◇ ◇ ◇

I am amazing. I am capable of extraordinary things. When I put my mind to anything, I can accomplish it. I know I am my own biggest critic, and today I break up with my self-blame. There is nothing wrong with me. There is nothing to fix. I am extraordinary. I make a difference in everyone's lives because I am gift to this world.

◇ ◇ ◇ ◇

How can I celebrate my awesome self?

IT IS TIME TO SAY GOOD-BYE TO THE LIFE I KNOW—I LET MYSELF GROW.

Chances are you are feeling anxiety because you are holding on to aspects of your life that no longer work as well as they used to. Repeat the mantra "I say good-bye to the life I know because I know it is time to grow." There is great growth waiting for you, but it requires you to take the first step forward, which is to release what no longer works. Now is the time to let go. You will be protected and guided through the transition—opportunity awaits.

◇ ◇ ◇ ◇

I am safe and secure. I take a step forward and honor the inspiration in my heart. I am walking into the next phase of my life with courage, joy, and ease. All is in right order.

◇ ◇ ◇ ◇

What do I want for my life?
Who do I want to be?

NOT EVERYTHING IN MY LIFE
DESERVES MY ATTENTION.

Everything is energy. What we spend time doing and who we spend our time with are either contributing to our well-being or taking away from it. You can learn the power of protecting your energy and owning your worth by becoming more aware of your own energy and what you are giving extra attention to. Spend it only on what is worth your time. Your future self will thank you.

◇ ◇ ◇ ◇

I protect myself by aligning with joy, love, and light. I protect my energy by giving my time to the things that make me feel good. I no longer give my energy to anything that feels heavy, dramatic, negative, or harmful. I am healthy. I am safe. I am secure.

◇ ◇ ◇ ◇

What have I been giving extra energy to that no longer feels good to me?

WHAT I'M SEARCHING FOR IS NOT OUT THERE—IT IS IN ME.

Having unrealistic expectations prevents us from moving forward. It's hard to stay motivated if you're constantly being disappointed. Having a vision is crucial, but giving yourself unrealistic goals is a trick the ego sometimes plays to prevent you from going outside of your comfort zone. See, the ego is reacting to fear—while its goal is to try to keep us safe, it often keeps us stuck instead. Instead of focusing on how your expectations aren't being met, can you shift your attention to an outcome that feels more joyful? This will allow freedom and playfulness back into your creative process.

◇ ◇ ◇ ◇

I let go of my outward desires and look inward to see that all my needs are always meet. I have everything I need inside of me. From this place of expectance, I will feel more balanced and fulfilled.

◇ ◇ ◇ ◇

What expectation has kept me from enjoying my life?

I EVOLVE ACCORDING TO MY OWN REACTION TO EACH SITUATION.

When situations happen that cause you unease, it can be easy to fall into fear or anger and overreact. But to truly grow and evolve, turn your reactions into a more loving intention. When you can step aside and see the big picture, you will see that your emotions sometimes get in the way of moving forward. There is a time and place for our feelings, but reacting to situations before we think about the big picture can prevent us from moving through the situation and healing it. Next time a troubling outcome occurs, do your best to align with love and compassion versus overreacting. This will help you learn the lessons available to you and rise above the drama.

◇ ◇ ◇ ◇

My life is like a classroom, and I am learning lessons every day. I choose to see the lessons and graduate to the next level or awareness. I do this by actively focusing on the big picture. I do not need to emotionally react to circumstances I cannot control. Instead, I use compassion, love, and light to learn the lessons and move forward. My growth is essential to my happiness, and I evolve according to my reaction to each situation and how I perceive it all with more love.

◇ ◇ ◇ ◇

What situation have I recently overreacted to?
How can I be calmer when addressing this issue?

I TAKE A LEAP OF FAITH.

Having faith will serve you well right now. You may have a goal or dream and be unsure of how to proceed. You must believe in yourself and hold faith that it is possible. When you lead from your heart, you will be guided with love. Take a leap and move forward with your dreams. Taking a leap of faith also relates to a new relationship and romantic love. If you are unsure of your path forward, trust your heart and jump into the experience.

◇ ◇ ◇ ◇

I remove all fear of the unknown, and I comfortably take a leap into my future. I am being guided with love, and the Universe supports my desires. There is nothing to fear, for all is in the right order.

◇ ◇ ◇ ◇

Where can I take a leap of faith?

MY LIFE GETS BETTER WHEN I PUSH THROUGH MY COMFORT ZONE.

What have you always wanted to do but have yet to give a go? Your comfort zone may need some stretching. You might be comfortable doing things a specific way, and a routine can feel safe and predictable. Stepping out of your comfort zone will bring fresh life and energy to your routine. Revisit your dreams from childhood days. What have you always wanted to do? Now is the time to go for it.

◇ ◇ ◇ ◇

I embrace new opportunities with excitement and wonder. I follow through on my dreams by stepping out of my current routine. I step out of my comfort zone, which helps me grow and change. My dreams matter, and I go after them with gusto.

◇ ◇ ◇ ◇

Where can I stop playing it safe?

ALL MY FEARS ARE FANTASY.

When you listen to your fears, your life may feel unmanageable. When we let fear run the show, it creates false illusions and separates you from others. Fear is based on stories in your mind that can harm you and others. Fear clouds your judgment and prevents you from making smart choices. To recognize your fear, say, "My fear is not real. I choose love."

◇ ◇ ◇ ◇

When I pay attention to my fears, they create new realities for me. I choose to disengage from all fear-based thoughts, and I return to love. Love will guide me into my real dream life, one guided by support and positive action.

◇ ◇ ◇ ◇

What fear do I believe that is most outrageous?

I AM WHO I NEEDED WHEN I WAS YOUNGER.

My dear, lovely you, your inner child is crying. Your inner child is the you from years ago who is trying to stay safe and secure. We all have pieces of us stunted from childhood; we didn't get the love we needed or felt we deserved. We grow up trying to fill these unmet needs, but inside we are still hurting. Show up for yourself by giving yourself what you needed as a child: love, attention, and care. Be the person you needed when you were younger.

◇ ◇ ◇ ◇

I am who I needed when I was younger. I care for my inner child with love, compassion, and understanding. I forgive those who hurt me and let myself heal from the pain.

◇ ◇ ◇ ◇

What childhood wound or insecurity needs
to be healed?

FOLLOWING MY HEART IS THE MOST RESPONSIBLE THING I CAN DO FOR MY WELL-BEING.

How well do you feel? Gauging your wellness by how often you listen to your heart is a process you can cultivate. Your heart is a tool to help you feel and do your best. When you look at your life and see the things you enjoy and appreciate, it's evidence that your heart has been in the driver's seat of your decisions. If you look around and see situations you dislike, you can take responsibility for your own happiness and health and listen to your heart.

◇ ◇ ◇ ◇

I listen to my heart 100 percent of the time. I gauge my wellness by how much happiness I feel in my life. When I am happy, it is a reflection of my heart leading the way. I choose happiness, health, and wellness, and this comes from me listening to my heart.

◇ ◇ ◇ ◇

How can I be more responsible for my
own well-being?

Day 206

EVEN THE DARKNESS HAS ITS WONDERS.

There is beauty in the breakdown. When you are depressed or in a desperate place, wonder can be found in even this moment. Feel the emotions of this situation fully. Part of living a rich life is to feel each moment and accept what it offers. When you embrace the darkness, the light will come. Ask yourself what you can learn here and why you are experiencing this. Your inner voice will lead you through the darkness.

◇ ◇ ◇ ◇

I can see the light. Even in my darkest hour, I reach for hope. This helps me pull into a place of understanding and peace. I can overcome anything when I am present and focused. I rise above this pain to see the purpose. There is wonder in every moment of my life. I am present for the experience.

◇ ◇ ◇ ◇

What purpose can I see in my current pain?

THERE IS ONLY ONE ME.

You may feel lonely because you are trying to fit in. You are not made to fit in. You are unique and special as you are. Pay attention to your thoughts about other people as well. Do you compare yourself to others? When you look at others in relation to your own life, you may think they have more or are more successful than you. When you compare yourself to others, it separates you from love. It also prevents you from feeling your true worth. Instead of looking at others and comparing them to yourself, focus on how unique you are.

◇ ◇ ◇ ◇

I am special and unique as I am. It does not serve me to compare myself to other people because everyone is special in its own unique way. I want to be me, and I have no desire to be like anyone else. My life is my own to create, so I actively celebrate myself and all I can do.

◇ ◇ ◇ ◇

To whom can I stop comparing myself?

THE MORE ME I SHOW,
THE MORE MY LIFE WILL FLOW.

Most of us don't want to move forward unless we know it will work out. Ironically, if we don't act, we will naturally produce the outcome we fear most. Just take one step at a time. Each step will build to something much bigger, but your life will only feel good if you show up more fully for you. The more you can show, the easier it will be to get what you want when you want. By being honest and revealing your true self, you will soon see the world loving you for who you are instead of who you think you need to be.

◇ ◇ ◇ ◇

I accept who I am and am proud of how far I've come. I show up daily in my life by taking care of me and showing my authentic truth. The more me I show, the easier things are in my life. I no longer hide behind false realities and instead show my true, authentic, beautiful self.

◇ ◇ ◇ ◇

Where can I be more honest with myself?

WHEN I HEAL MYSELF, I HELP TO HEAL THE WORLD.

Have you ever noticed that "healthy self" can be broken in a different place to spell "heal thyself?" This is a profound recognition that you must undergo a healing journey as you return to your whole self: one of love, kindness, and compassion. You are healing and growing, and as you continue to show up for the healing process, recognize that you are impacting the world in a positive way. When you heal yourself, you create waves of positivity that help impact the world.

You are not required to change all at once. You are asked to be brave enough to take one small step at a time. Little by little, each of these changes will lead to massive transformation. So instead of asking yourself, "How can I make a life change?" ask yourself to be courageous enough to move ahead without knowing.

◇ ◇ ◇ ◇

I am patient and kind to myself as I heal and grow. There is no destination or outcome to my healing journey, for being in the process is where the true transformation happens. I heal myself, and as I do, I help to heal the world.

◇ ◇ ◇ ◇

Which part of me needs the most healing right now?

I CAN REINVENT MYSELF AT ANY TIME.

It is never too late to be what you wanted for yourself. You can change directions and start fresh at any time. Part of the joy of life is expressing yourself and trying new things. If your heart is calling you to change careers, try a new hair color, or move to a new country, follow this impulse. It is not rash or inappropriate. It is your mission. That constant feeling that something is missing will disappear when you give yourself permission to reinvent yourself and try new things.

◇ ◇ ◇ ◇

I have ideas dear to my heart. I confidently express these ideas and share them with the world. It is always the right time to change course and try new things. I experience my life fully, which means I dive into all of my heart's callings with positive energy and a willingness to succeed.

◇ ◇ ◇ ◇

How can I reinvent myself?

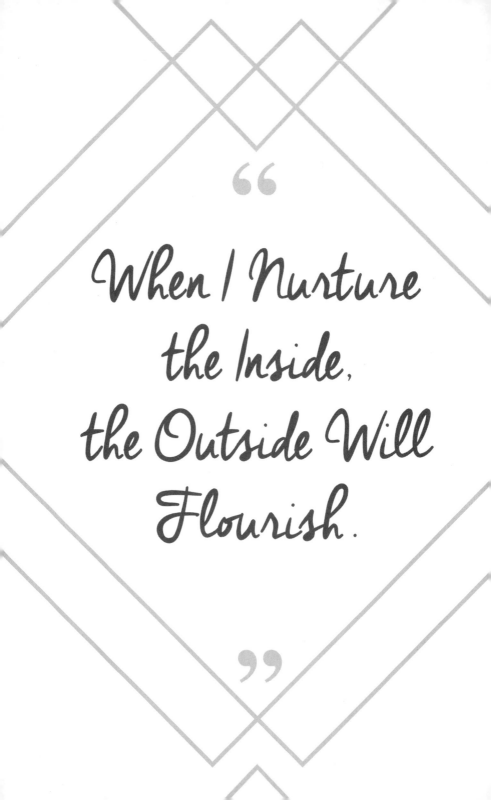

"

When I Nurture
the Inside,
the Outside Will
Flourish.

"

WHEN I NURTURE THE INSIDE, THE OUTSIDE WILL FLOURISH.

Healthy is not a one-size-fits-all. You may be putting too much pressure on yourself to look a certain way. The benchmark for your optimal health is to focus on how you feel. When you take care of yourself and focus on caring for your inner world, your outside will flourish. How you talk to yourself about yourself is important too. Don't let your inner critic tell you that you need to change to be happy. This is a trick the ego plays. Instead, focus on all the wonderful things you are doing to care for yourself. Say kind things to yourself and focus on self-care. As you do this with more intent and consistency, you will see your life transform.

◇ ◇ ◇ ◇

I focus on caring for myself in beautiful ways that feel good. I align with activities, people, foods, and situations that are nurturing, kind, and supportive to my overall goals. I remove negativity and take pride in myself daily.

◇ ◇ ◇ ◇

In what ways can I nurture myself more?

I DO ONE THING EVERY DAY FOR WHICH MY FUTURE SELF WILL HUG ME.

You are in control of your life and the outcome. Yes, there is a balance of fate and freewill, but if you sit back and let life happen to you, you will miss opportunities for you to become what you desire. Instead of waiting on happiness or for things to fall into place, start to create an action plan for your life. Create a big-picture goal and do at least one thing every day for which your future self will hug you.

◇ ◇ ◇ ◇

I embrace my life as a creative endeavor. I jump in with both feet. I do not wait for happiness. I go out and create my life adventure. I show up for my future self by taking steps today to get me where I want to go. I am in control of my life.

◇ ◇ ◇ ◇

What action step can I take today for which
my future self will hug me?

Day 213

I CREATE MY OWN
EXTRAORDINARY REALITY.

Filmmaker and philosopher, Jason Silva, said it best: "Once we realize the extraordinary power we have to compose our lives, we'll move from passive, conditioned thinking to being cocreators of our fate." You get to become what you want. But there are no quick fixes, no magic bullets. There are only the small, consistent, smart actions you can take every day that, compounded over time, will create unstoppable momentum. Sometimes you're not supposed to see the entire path. If you're creating it, you can only know what's next.

◇ ◇ ◇ ◇

I believe in what feels good, and aligning myself with what I want is what brings me the most joy. Instead of focusing on what I don't want, I spend my time creating and actively pursuing what I know will bring me joy.

◇ ◇ ◇ ◇

What kind of life do I truly want to live?

I AM CONFIDENT IN BELIEFS THAT WORK FOR ME.

Others may have beliefs or opinions that conflict with yours. This may cause stress or arguments. There is nothing to change about other people who have contrasting opinions. The differences in life make it rewarding. Without other people's points of view, you would not understand your own so clearly. Instead of turning to arguments or judgment, align with your own beliefs and why you feel the way you do. You don't need to prove other people wrong. When you are comfortable with what you stand for, you can exemplify your values. You don't need to tell people what you care about. You can show them.

◇ ◇ ◇ ◇

I refuse to argue my beliefs in order to get others to believe me. I am confident in my understanding of my self and all I stand for. The beliefs that work for me are part of my own rewarding journey and I respect that others have their own paths. I connect with my own sense of self by showing people what I care about instead of telling them.

◇ ◇ ◇ ◇

What can I show people instead of telling them?

Day 215

I COMMIT TO STAYING OPEN-MINDED.

When you are afraid, you close yourself off to loving outcomes. Use this time to practice surrender and to deepen your faith in the bigger picture. From a spiritual perspective, everything is always in right order. If you can't accept what is, you work to change it. But do so with grace, love, and intention. Through the process, stay open-minded and be open to new outcomes. You may not understand why others do what they do, but when you have an open mind and open heart, it will soon make sense.

◇ ◇ ◇ ◇

When I align with my truth, I am always on the right track. I stay open in the journey, and I am willing to live my life in new ways. I see opportunities where struggles used to be. I open my mind and heart to love more and am more accepting of others.

◇ ◇ ◇ ◇

What situation can I accept more?

NO ONE ELSE KNOWS WHAT'S BEST FOR ME.

Have you been second-guessing yourself or asking other people for their opinions about your life? Ask yourself if this is serving you. When you ask others for their opinions, it is because you are unsure. But when you get to the heart of the situation, you always know what is best for yourself. No one else knows how you should live your life. Do yourself a favor and stop trusting everyone else's opinions. Instead, trust your own.

◇ ◇ ◇ ◇

I trust myself and listen to my inner voice. I do not need to ask others for advice because I know what is right for me. I trust my own guidance and listen to it with an open mind. I know what is best for me. My heart is my compass.

◇ ◇ ◇ ◇

What advice have I recently asked for from another person when I already knew the answer?

WHAT I SEE IN OTHERS IS A REFLECTION OF MYSELF.

When you look at others with judgment, you are judging yourself. What we see in others is a reflection of our own position in life. Instead of reacting or blaming others, ask yourself what each situation brings up for you. If another person is rude, but you feel you are kind, ask yourself where you are rude in your life. You may be surprised to find you are disrespectful and talk down to yourself. When you are accountable for your reflections, you can align with love and positive light.

◇ ◇ ◇ ◇

I am accountable for all my feelings. Instead of attacking others, I look inward with curiosity. I know I am a mirror for others and what I dislike about them is something within myself that needs attention. I can choose to see what I see in others, and I focus on the good. I cultivate more loving relationships, being kind and compassionate to myself first.

◇ ◇ ◇ ◇

What bothers me in another person?
How is this a reflection of myself?

WHEN I LOOK AT THE WORLD AS A GOOD, HAPPY, AND KIND PLACE, GOOD, HAPPY, AND KIND THINGS COME TO ME.

Your experience of the world is largely affected by how you see the world. You will empower yourself by focusing on what you want to see and experience. Look at what you believe in and see if that is reflected in your life. Focus your energy into feeling positive thoughts and believe the world is on your side. When you believe people and the world are good, you will see evidence of this in your everyday life. Happiness comes to those who open up to seeing happiness as possible for them.

◇ ◇ ◇ ◇

I deserve to be happy and healthy. I am kind and do everything with great love. I make choices from a loving place, and I give others the benefit of the doubt. I believe in the greater good of mankind, and I am part of peace. When I show up happy, kind, and from a good-feeling place, this is reflected in every experience of my life.

◇ ◇ ◇ ◇

What kind, loving thoughts can I project out into the world?

I AM WORTH IT, AND I HAVE A LOT TO GIVE.

You have so much to give this world and other people. When you share your opinions, views, ideas, and self with vulnerability and honesty, people fall in love with you. The more true to yourself you are, the more others can get to know you. If you only show a side of you that is a version of what you think they want to see, you do yourself and others a disservice. By being true to yourself, you give the true you to the world. You share an honest reflection of yourself, which invites authentic connections into your life.

◇ ◇ ◇ ◇

I am true to myself by being my real self. I don't hide behind masks or false versions of me. I am proud and confident in the person I have become. I am worth it, and I have a lot to give this world. My ideas are respected, and I am admired for my transparency.

◇ ◇ ◇ ◇

Where can I give more of my real self?

I DON'T WASTE TIME WITH NEGATIVE THOUGHTS.

You and your life are far too precious for negative thoughts. Stop spending time thinking about what you dislike about yourself and start to celebrate the true beauty that you are. Instead of overthinking situations with negative thoughts, see the situations you dislike with more love. Send love to your insecurities and troubling situations and watch how they transform. You will soon feel more peace and ease.

◇ ◇ ◇ ◇

I do not waste any time with negative thoughts. I focus all my energy on what is going well, and I celebrate the good in my life and the world. There is no darkness where there is light, and I am the light. I shine forward with love.

◇ ◇ ◇ ◇

What negative thought could I flood with love?

MY LIFE GETS BETTER BY CHANGE, NOT CHANCE.

People make changes in their lives in two ways: by fear and desperation or by inspiration. When you make choices from a heartfelt place, you will grow into new beginnings with love and grace. If you make changes out of fear, you are still cultivating new experiences and growth opportunities, but the energy may feel more challenging. No matter what, your life gets better through active change.

You can wait for your life circumstances to change, but this does not happen by chance. Everything you have ever done in your life is part of an orchestrated plan. You get to conduct your masterpiece. When you put everything you have learned into play, you create deep, rich experiences that reward your soul. Change in your life comes from you taking action.

◇ ◇ ◇ ◇

I make calculated moves forward in my life to create positive change. My life is ever-changing, and I am in flow. I embrace change as though I have chosen it myself, because I have. Everything I experience is my choice and I choose, to make choices from inspiration and love.

◇ ◇ ◇ ◇

What change can I make today?

KINDNESS WINS.

Don't take offense to what others say and do. When people hurt you, choose kindness. When people love you, choose kindness. Kindness will always win. Be authentic with your expression of truth. This means choosing kindness is an option for all who seek internal love. If you are kind to your enemies and you mean it, you will feel more love in your life. Kindness is not something you want to force or pretend. Smiling when you don't feel like it is not the act of a kind heart. When you live your life by embracing love, kindness will naturally be your way of life.

◇ ◇ ◇ ◇

I am kind in the face of negativity. I choose my battles, and that helps me overcome all challenges. I do not engage in negative activity, and I release all judgment of others. I demonstrate peace by showing the world my kindness. I live from my heart, which is full of peace and love. I am kind. Kindness wins.

◇ ◇ ◇ ◇

To whom can I be kinder?

Day 223

WHEN I SPEAK MY TRUTH, IT GIVES OTHERS PERMISSION TO DO THE SAME.

You have an important point of view and message to share with others. When you speak your truth, you give others permission to do the same. Part of the healing process is to be able to openly share your story. When you speak your truth, you feel a gentle release, and peace can set in. What have you wanted to say but have been afraid of speaking up about? This is an opportunity for you to be honest with yourself and others—speak up and speak your truth.

◇ ◇ ◇ ◇

I am comfortable speaking up and sharing how I feel. I am confident in my situation and know that when I share openly and honestly, I am healing myself and helping others. The more I share my true self with others, the more loved I will feel. I give others permission to speak up when I speak my truth.

◇ ◇ ◇ ◇

What have I gone through that I can share with others to help them?

I DISENGAGE FROM ALL HARMFUL ACTIVITIES.

If you are going through a difficult situation, you might be trying to cope. It is natural for humans to turn to harmful substances, habits or addictions to help ease the burden of pain. Instead of blaming yourself or feeling guilty for turning to habits or activities that seem bad, embrace your true self with love. When you can love yourself even through your pain, it will be easier to disengage from harmful activities, people, and places. Do all things with love and you will be guided to recover more naturally.

◇ ◇ ◇ ◇

I am not my addictions or harmful habits. I choose to see myself in a temporary situation, and I release my need to numb myself through pain. I disengage from harmful people, places, and things by choosing love and letting love guide the way.

◇ ◇ ◇ ◇

What harmful activity can I stop doing?

I AM READY TO CHANGE AND EMBRACE NEW PATTERNS AND WAYS OF BEING.

Part of life is willingly accepting change as you embrace new ways of living. Today is a fresh start and an opportunity for you to release old patterns, habits, or thoughts that keep bringing you down. Set yourself up for success by creating a focused intention to help you step into the next phase of your life. Stay positive and focus on what you want.

◇ ◇ ◇ ◇

I am ready for change. I embrace new opportunities and am ready for growth. My life is constantly changing, and my journey is unfolding perfectly. I let go of what no longer resonates with me, and I step into my future with positive intention and a loving heart.

◇ ◇ ◇ ◇

What new habit can I start?

EVERY SITUATION IS AN OPPORTUNITY TO CHOOSE LOVE OVER FEAR.

You always have a choice. In every situation, you can choose love or you can choose fear. When you choose fear, you will feel constricted, anxious, overwhelmed, depressed, and even angry. If you embrace love, you will feel expansive, hopeful, happy, and at peace. Pay attention to how you feel. It will show you the way.

◇ ◇ ◇ ◇

I choose love in every situation of my life. I embrace the expansive nature of my true self and lead my life from my heart. When I am in fear, I turn to love by expressing my truth. I examine my fear and release it with compassion and love. I always choose love.

◇ ◇ ◇ ◇

What fear can I replace with love?

ALL IS IN THE RIGHT ORDER.

There is a perfect timing to everything in your life, including where you live. If you find yourself worried about your future or trying to figure out how what you want can happen, relax in the moment and see that where you are is perfect. The more we focus on our tomorrow, the less we can enjoy today. There are certain aspects of your life that are unfolding, so patience is needed as you assess where you are, so you can get to where you want to be. Keep focusing on what you want, and the clarity will pull you forward. You are like a farmer planting seeds that will soon grow into your manifested desires. Trust the process.

◇ ◇ ◇ ◇

I am comfortable in the present moment. I accept where I am and actively pursue my goals with more intention and focus. I am exactly where I am supposed to be; my life is unfolding into the master plan I have created.

◇ ◇ ◇ ◇

What current situation can you accept
and surrender to?

Day 228

PASSION IS MY PURPOSE—IT LEADS ME FORWARD.

Your lack of clarity is only an illusion. It may feel debilitating and can cause anxiety, but the lack of purpose you feel isn't lack at all but an open space for you to get more clarity. You may feel like you don't know what you want to do, but you do know what makes you happy. Follow through on the things that make you feel alive. Be honest with yourself and pursue your passions with gusto.

◇ ◇ ◇ ◇

I am a passionate person, and I focus on what brings me joy. I lead my life, feeling free to express my true self with creativity, wonder, and awe. I pursue my passions with focus and clear intentions and openly live a passion-filled life.

◇ ◇ ◇ ◇

What am I most passionate about?

LOVE IS THE KEY TO MY SUCCESS.

Have you heard that what you put into the world will come back to you? This is true on all levels. Sending positivity and love into the world will bring both back to you. Love is the key to your success and desires. When you approach your life with love, you will see reflections of all you desire on its way to you.

The Universe is full of loving support to guide you to your true purpose. When you do everything with love, you will shine brightly for the world to see your true light. Love has no bounds, no enemies, and no borders. Choose love and make it an everyday part of life.

◇ ◇ ◇ ◇

I am love. Everything I do is an indication of my love for myself and the world. I am connected to my world by showing love in each moment. I have no shame or judgment, no denial or self-doubt. Love is all there is. Love is all there will ever be. I am love. I do all things with great love.

◇ ◇ ◇ ◇

What small thing can I add great love to?

Day 230

I PAUSE IN MY PLEASURE.

You may feel as though you are alive but not really living. Perhaps you are going through the motions and not engaged with your life. One way to dive deeper into your life and feel the love is to pause in the pleasure. Each day offers abundant opportunities for you to feel joy and passion. Whether it is eating a fresh orange, drinking your morning latte, driving with your windows down, or hugging your dear friend, pleasurable moments happen all the time. When you can pause in each moment, your life becomes more rich and rewarding. Challenge yourself to pause and soak in what life has to offer.

◇ ◇ ◇ ◇

Taking time to be in each moment of my life will expand my happiness infinitely. I pause in the moments that offer me great pleasure. My life is enriched with multiple rewards. I am present, focused, and alive. I pause and take great pleasure in the simple joys of my life.

◇ ◇ ◇ ◇

What pleasure can I pause in?

REGRETS ARE OPPORTUNITIES TO LEARN AND GROW.

Each experience of your life is an opportunity to learn more about yourself and those around you. When you focus on what went wrong or what might have been, you keep yourself out of the experience of life. When you hold on to regrets, you are causing harm to yourself. It's like saying to yourself, "I made a mistake. I am damaged." But regrets are just areas of our lives that call for more attention. What is it about the situation that caused you frustration or guilt? Go into your regrets and ask what you learned.

◇ ◇ ◇ ◇

All of my regrets are actually opportunities for growth. I learn from all my regrets by being present in my life. I actively remove my worries by looking at my past and asking myself what I learned. I live a regret-free life because every regret helped me learn more about myself.

◇ ◇ ◇ ◇

What recent regret have I learned from?

Day 232

YOU KNOW THE TRUTH BY THE WAY YOU FEEL.

My dear, there are so many amazing, wonderful, beautiful, extraordinary things on their way to you. It is as if the entire Universe has conspired to bring you the abundance of fulfillment you so desire. Hold on to this vision that everything you want and need will come to you at the exact right time. The Universe is full of miraculous moments, blessings that surround you all the time. Instead of focusing on what currently is not working in your life, focus your attention on all that you want to be, feel, and have. Express your true self by aligning your energy with the abundant Universe and its ever-flowing blessings.

◇ ◇ ◇ ◇

I appreciate all that I am now and all that I am becoming. I thank the Universe daily for its ever-expansive abundance and the unfolding of my desires. I choose to see the light in all situations and send my troubles more love. The pain I feel will be removed when I turn my attention to gratitude. All is always in the right order, especially when I focus on the blessings in my life and thank the Universe for the blessings I don't even know about yet.

◇ ◇ ◇ ◇

What recent blessing has happened that I can be
more grateful for?

I DON'T USE AVOIDANCE TACTICS.

Be honest with yourself. Do you ever depend on others but then blame them when they don't come through? When we attack people with negative energy, we hurt ourselves in the interactions. Avoiding the real issues will never allow you to be free of worry. Instead of blaming others or trying to solve problems by dancing around the issues that concern you, be straightforward and address them head on.

◇ ◇ ◇ ◇

I do not dance around the issues in my life. I am honest with others and myself, and when an issue arises, I address it openly. Other people respect me because I am honest with them. When I express my truth, I stand in integrity as I honor myself and my relationships with others.

◇ ◇ ◇ ◇

What relationship in my life needs more honesty?

I AM PATIENT WITH MYSELF.

Forgive yourself. Please don't be so hard on yourself. You are doing the best you can. When you are kind to yourself, you will feel more productive and successful. Instead of condemning yourself, be patient. The journey to your heart is a sacred adventure, one that takes time. It is a process of learning about yourself through the journey of life.

◇ ◇ ◇ ◇

I am learning and growing every day. I am patient with myself as I try new things. I am also kind to myself through the process of healing. On the journey to reaching my goals, I create a timeline that aligns with my highest good. Even when things don't happen when I want them to, I am patient, and I trust divine timing and myself.

◇ ◇ ◇ ◇

Where should I be more patient with myself?

I GIVE UP CONTROL.

You may want to control certain outcomes, and even people, in your life. It is natural for humans to want to feel safe, but when we control our environment, we create a false sense of security. Trying to maintain balance through controlling anything is never a way to achieve what you want. By giving up control and allowing others to support you and show up for you, you will feel more loved. Trusting the Universe is a large part of releasing the reins on your life. Hand over your worries and concerns to the Universe and you will be guided to love.

◇ ◇ ◇ ◇

I release my need to control my life and those in it. I turn my worries over to the Universe and know I am safe and secure. I release my need for approval of others, and I accept them as they are. I give up control of trying to know or figure out how things are supposed to work out. Instead, I navigate my own life adventure with grace and ease.

◇ ◇ ◇ ◇

Where can I give up control in my life?

I STAY ON PROJECTS UNTIL I SEE A SUCCESSFUL CONCLUSION.

Don't give up on your dreams or projects. Today is a reminder that all things take time and will manifest at their own pace. Instead of rushing a project or quitting before it is complete, pull yourself into the journey of the project and find the fun. Great joy can be found in the creation process. Instead of focusing so much on the end result, how can you be more in the process?

◇ ◇ ◇ ◇

I don't give up on projects. I am accountable for my life, and I successfully see things through until the end. When I align my heart and head, I am unstoppable. Everything I touch is golden. My projects are full of love, and I complete them with joy.

◇ ◇ ◇ ◇

What details of a project or goal do I need
to focus on more?

Day 237

I GIVE OTHERS THE BENEFIT OF THE DOUBT.

You have a choice. You can trust people the first time you meet them, or you can distrust them until they earn it. When you give people the benefit of the doubt, you see the good and allow them to show you their true colors. There is no need to judge others for their actions or suspect they are being dishonest. Give them the benefit of the doubt and watch how your communication will deepen.

◇ ◇ ◇ ◇

I see the good in others. I give them the benefit of the doubt, and I leave my own issues out of situations. I approach each relationship nonjudgmentally and with an open mind. I believe in the good of others and trust their characters.

◇ ◇ ◇ ◇

Who can I forgive and give the benefit of the doubt?

THE LITTLE THINGS I DO MAKE A BIG DIFFERENCE.

You may feel like you are not making a big enough difference in your life. The quality of your life is not determined by how many people you help or heal or how big of a difference you make. It is determined by how many little things you do with great love.

Look at everyday little things, such as opening a door for a stranger, buying coffee for a friend, or helping a homeless person by giving money or food. These small acts of kindness can make a giant impact that will resonate forever. The little acts of kindness are more important than waiting for an opportunity to do some big, grandiose gesture. Give more attention to the mini moments that bring opportunities for support and love.

◇ ◇ ◇ ◇

I put extreme care into all I do. I make an impact in everyone's life because I am focused on the power of the present moment. I practice being present, and I help and support those in need. My desire to help is my greatest asset to happiness. When I do small things with great love, I am living my purpose.

◇ ◇ ◇ ◇

What little act of kindness can I do today?

MY SELF-RESPECT AND DIGNITY ARE MY TOP PRIORITY.

You must not stay in any relationship or situation that makes you feel less than the amazing person you are. Today is a reminder that you should be your own top priority. Look at all of your relationships and see where you are sacrificing yourself to make another person happy. Focus on your own happiness by making yourself a priority.

◇ ◇ ◇ ◇

I am in the best relationship of my life—one with myself. I meet my needs with compassion and joy, and I am my top priority. I respect myself by removing all negative relationships and people from my life. I am kind, loving, and compassionate to myself, and my desires manifest with dignity.

◇ ◇ ◇ ◇

In what ways can I make myself my top priority?

Day 240

I CAN LAUGH AT MYSELF.

Life can be stressful. It may feel as though you are stuck within a series of obstacles to overcome. Pay attention to your energy. Are you stuck in the mundane, worrying about every situation or wrongdoing? Maybe you are stressing about the controllable and uncontrollable outcomes of life. When you make your happiness dependent on external situations, you may fail to see the humor and raw honesty of life. There is no need to take yourself so seriously. Finding the humor in seemingly troubling situations can bring more joy into your life. When you can lighten up and laugh at yourself, you will feel truly free. A smile can transform any difficult situation.

◇ ◇ ◇ ◇

I am easy-going and carefree. I can laugh at myself and be free to look at situations in a lighthearted manner. Life is a joy and a fun journey. I laugh and can see the humor in all situations. I don't take myself too seriously.

◇ ◇ ◇ ◇

How can I lighten up a little more?

I EAT MY FOOD GUILT-FREE.

Food is love. It is a form of nourishment and source of energy for sustainability. However, you may feel guilty when you want certain types of food. It is common to feel as though you shouldn't want that chocolate cake or those french fries, especially if you want to be healthy. Society puts a lot of pressure on you to eat specific foods, and if you enjoy certain foods that are not in the category of what is considered healthy, you feel guilty. But imagine if there were no right and wrong and everything you ate was considered good for you. For today, pretend everything you put in your mouth is healthy. When you truly enjoy your food and practice conscious eating, this is possible. There is no need to resist or fight food. You can love yourself and your body by eating foods guilt-free.

◇ ◇ ◇ ◇

I take the pressure off of myself by eating all my food with love. I savor each bite and appreciate the flavors. Being present with my food has released the burden of guilt, so I can be free to be true to me. I eat what I want and listen to my body as guidance for when I am full. I am healthy, vibrant, and at my ideal body weight. I eat all food guilt-free.

◇ ◇ ◇ ◇

What food do I feel guilty eating?
How can I transform this guilt into love?

I AM GENEROUS WITH MY TIME AND ENERGY. I SUPPORT THOSE I LOVE.

You may feel burdened by your own life stress and demands, but this is a perfect time to reach out and support others. When you feel stuck or stale in your own life, this is usually an indication that something is missing. You have a natural desire to help others, and when you are generous with yourself by sharing your time, energy, resources, and love, you help yourself. You will feel more balanced and be more focused and happy.

◇ ◇ ◇ ◇

I give without expecting anything in return. I am generous with my own resources by sharing my time, money, energy, and love with those around me. I support those I love by sharing my own abundance. The Universe is abundant and supplies all my needs. I give unto others, so I can be true to myself.

◇ ◇ ◇ ◇

What friend can I support by giving my time?

Day 243

MY SELF-SABOTAGING HABITS HAVE A MESSAGE FOR ME. I LISTEN TO THE GUIDANCE.

You don't need to feel guilty or put yourself through pain. If you have addictions or habits you feel guilty about, don't resist them. Instead, go into them and ask why they are there. When you can listen to your own body's wisdom, you will see the reason for your self-sabotage and addictions. You may be using these habits as a crutch to avoid facing a painful issue in your life. Awareness is the key to transformation.

◇ ◇ ◇ ◇

I allow myself to heal through my awareness. I am in tune with my body's needs and my true desires. I look deeply into my habits with love and compassion. Everything I need to heal is right here inside of me.

I send white light to my body's pain and flood my being with love. I am peaceful and connected to my body's wisdom. I listen to the guidance of my habits and transform them with love.

◇ ◇ ◇ ◇

What compassionate message does my self-sabotaging habit have for me?

I AM NOT POWERLESS.

You are not powerless. The entrapment you feel is not based on real information. Fear has created a shadow over your life and is making you feel stuck. You can always do something. Retreat into your heart and let your inner voice give you guidance. You will soon know the next right step for you to make as you move forward. You are never alone. A large support system is waiting to help you. Just ask for guidance and you will receive the support you need.

◇ ◇ ◇ ◇

I am not powerless. I make choices from a loving place, and I connect to my heart for guidance. I have a choice and I embrace love. My energy is full of love, and I release all fears. I am not trapped. I can move forward and free myself from this pain.

◇ ◇ ◇ ◇

Where do I feel powerless?
What can I do to move forward?

"

I Am
Not Powerless.

"

I START EACH DAY WITH A GRATEFUL HEART.

Think about how you woke up this morning. Were you frantic, focused on getting into the day and in a hurry? Or did you take a deep breath, soak in the new day's life, and stretch, say a prayer or maybe engage in meditation, and give thanks?

When you wake up with a grateful heart, your entire day unfolds more smoothly. Try it out. When you wake up, before you even open your eyes, give thanks. Declare to the Universe, God, your higher power, your angels, your dog, the air, or your significant other what you are thankful for.

◇ ◇ ◇ ◇

I am thankful for another day to be alive. I am thankful for my health and my happiness. I love my bed and my home, and I feel safe and secure. I am grateful for the beautiful world we live in. I can't wait to live my day. I am excited for life and eager to see how my day unfolds. I release the need to control anything. Instead, I am having fun along my journey of life.

◇ ◇ ◇ ◇

How can I cultivate a morning gratitude practice?

I STOP WORRYING HOW IT WILL HAPPEN AND START TRUSTING THAT IT WILL HAPPEN.

My dear, you are far too worried about the outcome. You are spending too much time obsessing, hoping, wishing, and focusing on the way in. What you want to happen will unfold. Instead of worrying and letting the anxiety eat you alive, focus on your faith. Now is not the time to abandon yourself by leaning into lack and what isn't happening. There are many things happening behind the scenes, and you're being guided to the next right step to help you move into new phases of your life. Stop worrying about the how and start trusting that what you want will happen at the exact right time and place.

◇ ◇ ◇ ◇

Everything happens in my life for my highest good. I understand that what I want will happen in its perfect time and place. All is in the right order. I turn my lack of faith into love by focusing on the wonderful things that are happening. There are many blessings I experience daily, and I choose to appreciate where I am instead of where I think I need to be.

◇ ◇ ◇ ◇

Where have I been overthinking and obsessing
about controlling the outcome?
How can I turn my fear into faith?

I AM RESPONSIBLE FOR CHANGING MY BEHAVIOR UNTIL I GET WHAT I WANT.

If you are frustrated with the outcome of recent actions, try again. Your life is an expansive unfolding of lots of experiments. Some experiments work, others do not. Part of living a rich, fulfilling life is being fully present in your journey. This means you are responsible for all you see. If you don't like the results, then change your behavior until you get what you want. Approach your life as an experiment. To get the results you want, keep changing your behavior until you find what works.

◇ ◇ ◇ ◇

I am responsible for my experience of life. I choose to focus on the results I want to see instead of dwelling on what didn't work in the past. I approach my life with open arms, and I behave my way to success.

◇ ◇ ◇ ◇

What behavior can I shift to try to get new results?

I STOP WORRYING ABOUT DEBT.

Having debt is one thing. Worrying about it is a completely different situation. You may have financial debt, and this can cause a strain on your relationships and your self-worth. Focusing on the debt causes tremendous pain, and it can actually prevent you from getting out of debt.

When you focus on the problem, the problem persists. Instead, focus on a solution. Take action steps to consolidate your loans and debt and make a plan to pay it off each month. Focusing on the solution to any problem will get you faster results than dwelling on the problem.

◇ ◇ ◇ ◇

There is no need to worry about financial debt. I am comfortable with myself, and I know the Universe is abundant. I release my lack mentality and allow money to flow to me. I actively work to pay off my debt by focusing on a solution. I take all my attention off of what is not working, so I can focus on what is. A payment plan helps me control my finances and release the worry.

◇ ◇ ◇ ◇

By what date will I be debt-free?
(Set a date to help empower yourself.)

I FORGIVE EX-LOVERS.

Holding on to past relationships after they expire is part of healing a broken heart. Love is love, and it can never die, though the form of the love changes and you may no longer be with the person you once loved. When you hold on to emotions and replay negative aspects of the relationship, you put yourself in a holding pattern of anger. Releasing that anger and letting go of regret will help you welcome in a new start.

Forgiving your ex-lovers doesn't mean saying what happened is okay. It just means you have accepted the situation and can now see the big picture. When you forgive, it is not about the other person. It is about you opening up your future because you have finally forgiven your past.

◇ ◇ ◇ ◇

I forgive you. You and I were part of a sacred plan that both of our souls signed on for. You taught me valuable lessons about life and myself. I never meant to hurt you, and the pain I feel is because you will always have a place in my heart. I forgive you. I wish you well. I release this energetic hold and trust happiness and health is on its way to you. Thank you for being in my life and helping me become more of who I really am. I am forever grateful for our time together. You will have a place in my heart forever.

◇ ◇ ◇ ◇

Who can I forgive?

Day 250

WHEN I HELP OTHERS, I HELP MYSELF.

Perhaps recent events have caused you to worry about the state of the world. You may feel powerless and hopeless. When you are overwhelmed with worry, it makes it difficult to feel happiness. You may feel like you don't matter and nothing you do will really help, but even one small act of kindness can help thousands of people.

If you feel as if something is missing in your life, it could be your connection to others. You may be trying to find happiness in activities and outside circumstances, but it still eludes you. When you chase happiness, it can never reach you. Instead, focus on how you can help others. Just donating time, money, or energy to a cause you care about will help you feel more grounded. If you are sad and consumed with worry, volunteer and help another person or charity. You can adopt a pet or find ways to help others. This has a profound impact on you increasing your own happiness. When you help others, you help yourself.

◇ ◇ ◇ ◇

True happiness comes when my words and actions help others. I enjoy giving my time, energy, and resources to help those in need. My problems may feel overwhelming, but when I get out of my own way and help other people, I end up helping myself. There is a power in me supporting another person. It helps me become less focused on my own pain and put things into perspective. When I help others, I help myself.

◇ ◇ ◇ ◇

What friend or family member can I help?

IT IS OKAY NOT TO BE OKAY.

Your anxiety may be filling your heart and flooding your mind. Right now it may feel impossible to move forward through all the mental chaos, but today is a reminder that you have a purpose here and your life is meant to be lived. Instead of feeling like something is wrong with you because you don't feel okay, recognize that part of living a balanced life is to embrace all of the uncertainty and emotions that come forth. Your emotions are valid even if they feel impossible. It is because you may be running from them, which often keeps you stuck. Let yourself be where you are instead of where you think you need to be. Repeat the mantra "I am okay, but I know it is okay not to be okay."

◇ ◇ ◇ ◇

I understand there are ups and downs to life, and I choose to be fully present for each situation as it happens instead of running or avoiding my feelings. I see the power of my emotions and know they are trying to tell me something. I embrace all that I am as I step forward through the uncertainty. I choose to be present and embrace this moment as it is.

◇ ◇ ◇ ◇

What emotions have I been afraid to feel?

Day 252

WHAT I WANT WANTS ME TOO.

Do not lose faith in yourself and your future. The Universe is working behind the scenes to manifest your heart's true desires. Now, more than ever, it is important to focus on what you want and believe it's on its way to you. What you want wants you too. Hold steady in the vision of your dreams coming forth, because they are closer than you realize.

◇ ◇ ◇ ◇

I am not off track and will not lose faith. I believe in my vision, and I know and trust that what I want wants me too. All is in the right order, and I am becoming who I need to be to receive what I truly need. I focus forward with intention, clarity, and faith. My faith is my focus as I lean into it with love and trust the power of my dream life manifesting into reality. All is in the right order.

◇ ◇ ◇ ◇

Where have I lost faith and given up on my dream?
How can I invite faith back into my life?

I SHOW THE WORLD MY WEIRD, CRAZY, BEAUTIFUL SELF.

Don't be afraid to show the world who you are. You may fear that people won't understand you or you won't fit in. But the truth is the more honest you are with yourself about who you are, the more the world can accept you. Challenge yourself to show the quirks and habits you hide. Be more honest with yourself by embracing your true self, the crazy in you. Your crazy is part of what others need to see so they don't feel so alone. Stop hiding yourself from the world and show off your beautiful, crazy, weird self.

◇ ◇ ◇ ◇

Nothing is standing in my way. I show up for myself by showing the world who I am. I embrace my quirky, weird, and funny characteristics. I don't have any habits I keep secret. I show people who I really am. When I do this, I get an honest reflection back. Because I am in love with myself and showing the world my true self, the world accepts and honors me as I am.

◇ ◇ ◇ ◇

What secretive habit can I share with others?

I INSPIRE OTHERS WITH MY OWN BIGNESS.

You have greatness inside you bigger than your body. All of your hopes and dreams are tucked deep in your soul. You are unlike anyone else in the world, which means you can inspire others just by being you. You may not feel confident or comfortable showing others your dreams or certain aspects of your personality, but this lack of confidence is usually tied to past experiences where shame was at play. Forgive your past and those who hurt you.

When you see how wonderful you are, you will release the confines of worry. Look at how much you have been able to accomplish in your life. Look at proof of your greatness in action. You are a superhuman who makes things happen. You have defied the odds and overcome turbulent times. Start singing the praises of your greatness. Take more risks because your greatness will support it.

◇ ◇ ◇ ◇

I am over being down on myself. I am sick of selling myself short. Today is a new beginning. I stand tall, confident, and proud of who I am. I choose to show the world my true self and all of my wonder. I am full of love and shining brightly from passion and purpose. I am great. I celebrate my greatness.

◇ ◇ ◇ ◇

Who inspires me with their own greatness?
Which of those qualities is reflected me?

I LIVE MY VALUES.

You have a power system ingrained in your soul. These are your personal values, the ones unique to you. No one else in the world has the same internal value system as you. When you identify and live your values, you will feel internal happiness. The Universe will reward you for being true to yourself, and your relationships, career, and life will flourish.

To identify your values, think about your childhood and what was most important to you. Helping others, expressing yourself creatively, moving your body with physical activity, such as dance, and so on. Your childhood is your source of inspiration because it represents you at your purest form. Identify and live your values for a happy approach to life.

◇ ◇ ◇ ◇

I am in love with my life. I live my values and show up with integrity in all my interactions. My values are a reflection of my soul's deepest desires. When I live from my heart, my values are effortless and in front-focus. My life is balanced, and I am happy because I set an example of what's possible. When I live my life by my own values, I guide others to do the same.

◇ ◇ ◇ ◇

What are my values?

I STAY HOPEFUL AND OPTIMISTIC IN DIFFICULT SITUATIONS.

Hope is your flashlight guiding you into happiness. When you are trapped by difficult situations, hope will guide you home. You always have what it takes to move through challenging times. It may feel as though there is no way out, but turning to hope will help you. You can focus on the positive aspects instead of the pain. Finding hope will help you overcome the troubling time.

When you feel a rush of excitement and worry-free energy, this is a signal you are grasping hope. Hope and optimism will be your compass, guiding you back to the light. Where there is love, there is always hope. Turn your fears over to the Universe and reach for love.

◇ ◇ ◇ ◇

I am hopeful in all areas of my life. I reach for good-feeling vibrations. I know difficult situations often bring great understanding of self-awareness, and I dive into my situations with attention on healing. I look for the good and see the positive aspects of each situation. I am aligned with my truth, which is love. I turn my fears over to the Universe. Love will guide me home.

◇ ◇ ◇ ◇

What can I be more optimistic about?

I SEE EVERYONE AS AN EQUAL.

Your relationships are the greatest opportunities for growth and understanding, which means the people in your life who cause the most emotional stress also offer the greatest opportunities for self-expansion. If someone in your life is causing you frustration, take a step back and see them as an equal. Having empathy for others will help expand your relationships.

If you are connected to an outcome or hoping another person will do what you want them to do, release this need for control. Everyone has their own set of struggles, beliefs, and situations they are going through. When you can release all judgment and let others be who they are, not who you think they should be, you will feel free.

◇ ◇ ◇ ◇

I do not play favorites or look at others with a discerning eye. I am committed to growing and show up with nonjudgmental energy. I see everyone as the same. We are all working through life together, navigating our own struggles. There is no need for me to reflect my pain onto others, nor do I take on theirs. Instead, I send love to everyone and accept that we are all equal.

◇ ◇ ◇ ◇

Who do I need to see as equal?

I ACCEPT THAT GOOD IS GOOD ENOUGH.

Stop working so hard trying to be perfect. Perfection is a silent killer that eats away your time, money, and energy. When you focus on perfection, you miss out on being in the process.

Accepting that sometimes good is good enough is the key to freedom and happiness. Give yourself permission to release the control and turn inward for self-acceptance. When you accept yourself, the actions and projects you create will always be good enough.

◇ ◇ ◇ ◇

I stop trying so hard to make sure everything is perfect. There is no need for me to work so hard to be perfect. The perfection is in the moment, and accepting that good is more than good enough is my real freedom. I let go of all the time I spend trying to make it perfect and see that others do not examine things the way I do. I am no longer hard on myself. I let go of control and celebrate the situation as it is.

◇ ◇ ◇ ◇

What situation can I stop trying to improve
and accept as good enough?

I AM COMFORTABLE SAYING THANK YOU.

It's nice to hear thank you. Other people in your life care deeply about you and want nothing but your happiness and health. When they reach out to do kind things for you, remember to say thank you. You may be thankful for things in your life and you may feel it, but today is a gentle reminder to cultivate the practice of verbalizing your thanks.

Giving thanks can be in the form of gifts, attention, time, money, and energy, but often the simplest thank you is just to say it. Saying thank you is a beautiful expansion of your human spirit. Being comfortable saying thank you helps those around you feel connected to you. You will see more love and appreciation when you can verbally share your gratitude.

◇ ◇ ◇ ◇

I wake up with a grateful heart and feel gratitude for all that is good. I love to show my appreciation for everything in my life by saying thank you. When I share my gratitude, others feel appreciated and respected. It is important for me to show what I am thinking. Appreciating others and their efforts is part of my own well-being. I give thanks openly and freely. When people pay me a compliment, I accept it with grace. I can accept compliments, and I give them freely. I am grateful for all in my life.

◇ ◇ ◇ ◇

Who has always been there for me that I can verbally
say thank you to?

I SET HIGH EXPECTATIONS.

Raising your standards is part of growing into your best self. When you start to show up for yourself and cultivate a practice of happiness, you will naturally raise your expectations. Setting high expectations is an opportunity for you to prove your own worth. You don't need to prove or show others anything. But by increasing your own standards, you show yourself how valuable you are. All areas of your life can have standards: your health, your relationships, your financial well-being, and your career. Look at every aspect of your life and ask yourself where you can set higher expectations.

◇ ◇ ◇ ◇

I matter. My life is a reflection of my goals manifested into action. I set high expectations for myself because it helps push me out of my comfort zone and reach new heights. By setting higher standards, I overcome new challenges and live a fuller life. I do not settle in any area of my life. I am aligned with my best self, and I set high expectations.

◇ ◇ ◇ ◇

Where can I set higher expectations?

Day 261

I AM RESILIENT.

Bouncing back from life's difficult situations is what you are a master at. It may feel like the situation you are currently in will never end, but this is a reminder of how resilient you are. You can and will overcome anything with grace and power. Align inward with your inner light and focus on the loving presence around you.

During difficult times, it's easy to feel like you are alone, but there is plenty of support and willingness to help around you. Be open to guidance and to receiving help. Your resilience is an asset that will carry you forward.

◇ ◇ ◇ ◇

I am so much stronger than I give myself credit for. I am an overcomer and achiever, a doer and a fighter. I can rise above any situation, with grace and power. I am resilient. When I am in difficult situations I reach out to the support around me. I let help in and allow those around me to help.

I overcome life's challenging moments because I am capable, willing, and strong. Every situation I experience is part of my greater understanding of life. I navigate through the difficult times with a strong determination and will to succeed. I can do this. I am an achiever. I am resilient.

◇ ◇ ◇ ◇

What have I bounced back from?

Day 262

SETBACKS DO NOT DEFINE ME. THEY NUDGE ME INTO A NEW AWARENESS.

Life is going smoothly, and then suddenly something comes along that throws us. When this happens, it seems like the Universe is conspiring against us just as everything was going right. However, setbacks in your life are not indications that you are off track. They are opportunities for more self-awareness and growth. The situation that feels the most difficult to navigate is often in your life as a teacher. Each situation that feels like a setback is actually realignment.

If you are honest with yourself, you can examine the outcome and see it is putting you on a path toward your highest good. When you go into each situation, ask yourself how it plays into your big picture. The experience in your life will no longer feel chaotic or random, and you will feel more grounded.

◇ ◇ ◇ ◇

I am peaceful. I am not attached to the outcomes of situations in my life. I feel connected to my purposes and see how everything works together. The recent setbacks in my life are actually opportunities for me to realign with my values and true worth. When I am honest with myself, I see there is no such thing as a setback. I am always being nudged into a new awareness of self. I am connected to my life, and I focus forward with love.

◇ ◇ ◇ ◇

What current situation feels like a setback but could actually be putting me back on track to my highest good?

I REWARD MYSELF WITH SIMPLE LUXURIES.

If you feel guilty for treating yourself, you are not alone. Most people want to make sure everyone else is cared for before it's time to care for themselves. For a balanced, happy, and peaceful life, reverse this approach. Instead of waiting for others to be happy before you can, put yourself first. One simple way to do this is to reward yourself with simple pleasures.

Little luxuries, like a chocolate bar or a bouquet of flowers, buying a nice outfit or candles for your bath, are all part of treating yourself well. Treating yourself to small special treats makes the journey more enjoyable. It helps you reconnect with yourself and feel more balanced.

◇ ◇ ◇ ◇

I treat myself to little gifts that bring me joy. I enjoy the process of investing in myself, for it reminds me I am loved. I care about my wellness and I show up for myself daily. My enjoying the simple luxuries reminds me that I make a difference in the world. When I take care of myself, I take care of others.

◇ ◇ ◇ ◇

What can I treat myself to today?

I LEAVE ALL UNHEALTHY SITUATIONS.

You most likely have been enduring a difficult situation for too long. The situation may be toxic and affecting your ability to be happy. You may have a hard time letting go because you have invested a lot of time, energy, and maybe even money. Ignoring the reality is hurting your health.

The experience you went through is itself the reward. The true benefit for your soul's growth will be revealed to you when you leave the unhealthy situation. Instead of looking at it as wasted energy and time, leave the unhealthy situation and free yourself. You can walk away without hesitation or guilt. Ask the Universe and friends for support that the parting is harmonious and for your highest good. But you know in your heart it is time.

◇ ◇ ◇ ◇

I leave all unhealthy situations and walk away with confidence and peace in my heart. I am doing the right thing, and all is in the right order. There is nothing here for me. It is time to leave.

I release my need to know the reason this situation was part of my life, for in time, this information will be revealed to me. I let go of everything unhealthy for me. I choose love. Healthy opportunities can now come my way.

◇ ◇ ◇ ◇

What unhealthy relationship will I let go of?

MY INNER VOICE IS TRUSTWORTHY.

You may be confused or feel uncertain. Today is verification that your inner voice is always speaking to you. You can trust the voice, for it will never lead you astray. Your heart speaks to you through your feelings, thoughts, and ideas, and you are hearing it accurately.

Pay attention to how you feel in each situation and trust your instincts. It is safe to move forward with changes in your life. Your inner voice is your guide, helping you navigate the transition.

◇ ◇ ◇ ◇

The feelings I feel are accurate and real. My inner voice is always talking to me. I trust the guidance and listen to it with an open heart and nonjudgmental awareness. I am secure in myself and connected to my heart's desires. I trust the voice within. It is my truth.

◇ ◇ ◇ ◇

What is my inner voice telling me?
How can I trust it more?

IT IS ALREADY DONE.

You will be pleased with the outcome. The Universe is working on your behalf to solve the problem. The Universe is working on a plan beyond your scope of human understanding. You may not see evidence of things working out but trust that the Universe has solved your troubling situation. Everything has already worked out. There is no need to carry the burden that things won't fall into place. Trust that the Universe has already taken care of your situation, so you can move forward with the confidence that you will get what you need.

◇ ◇ ◇ ◇

I am excited about the opportunities in my future. Everything is falling into place. Nothing is out of order. The Universe has created a master plan, and my desires are in motion. Everything I need is on its way to me. It is already done. There is nothing to worry about.

◇ ◇ ◇ ◇

In what situation can I hand my worries over to the Universe and trust they will be taken care of?

I DETACH FROM ALL TROUBLING SITUATIONS AND SURROUND THEM WITH LOVE.

You may be in a situation causing you pain. You are so embodied in the experience that you can no longer see it objectively. Look carefully at the big picture and surround yourself with love. Take the emotion out of the situation and see it is not about you. You can take the attachment out by depersonalizing the situation and objectively observing the outcome.

There is no need to take offense to others' behaviors. The situation is clouded with fear and judgment. When you give yourself permission to take time away and detach, you will see it more clearly. The objective point of view will help you though this situation.

◇ ◇ ◇ ◇

I refrain from judgment or seeing painful situations with fear. I detach myself from the experience and allow love to come in. Instead of looking at what others are doing wrong, I send them love and light for healing. When I detach from the situation, I am at peace, and the situations can heal.

◇ ◇ ◇ ◇

What situation can I remove myself from?

I GO FOR WHAT I WANT, NOT JUST WHAT I THINK IS POSSIBLE.

Pay attention to your thoughts. If you're settling into what you think is possible, you may be selling yourself short. You might be basing your potential off of failed opportunities or mistakes from your past. When you think about reaching your goals, do you go for what you want or settle for what you assume is possible? Make sure you are reaching for the stars and giving yourself permission to dream big. The Universe will support you in reaching your goals, but setting a clear intention is essential. Let the dreams that live inside your heart lead the way.

◇ ◇ ◇ ◇

I go for what I want in life, and I get it. I dream big and act out my goals. I don't settle nor do I sink into self-sabotage or doubt. I go for what I want, not just what is possible. I know that when inspiration comes, it is my mission to act on it. The dreams that come to me are part of my sacred contract. I go for what I want and live my dreams daily.

◇ ◇ ◇ ◇

Where can I dream bigger and actually go for what I want, instead of settling for what I think I can get?

OPPORTUNITIES FLY AT ME.

Position yourself to believe opportunities are everywhere. You will get results based on your expectations. When you expect good things to happen, you will see evidence in the making. Instead of focusing on problems, become solution-focused and see the opportunities around you. There is always something you can do, another possibility to try. Go for what you want and seek out support to help you get what you want. The Universe is supporting you and will deliver what you desire.

◇ ◇ ◇ ◇

I hold faith that everything is in perfect order. Opportunities are everywhere, and I am abundant and secure. My life is a reflection of my positive thoughts, and I see the results of my actions. I am living my dream life with new opportunities on the horizon. I celebrate all I am becoming and seek out new opportunities as they come.

◇ ◇ ◇ ◇

What opportunities can I embrace?

Day 270

I AM A "WHY NOT" PERSON.

There are two types of people in the world: the "why not" people and the "why bother" people. When it comes to making your dreams come true, embrace the "why not" attitude. If you say "why bother," then you sell yourself short. There will be many opportunities for you to give up on your dream. Don't. Fear and self-doubt will try to sabotage your efforts. Your mission is to keep moving forward with a can-do attitude. Embrace the "why not" and you will reach your goal.

◇ ◇ ◇ ◇

I do not allow my fears to derail me. When I get inspiration, I act on it with a "nothing is impossible" attitude. Instead of turning to why bother, I embrace the idea that anything is possible. When I put my mind to it, I can accomplish anything. There are no limitations accept those I put on myself.

◇ ◇ ◇ ◇

What dream can I go for?

"

I Am Always
on the Edge
of My Potential.

"

I AM ALWAYS ON THE EDGE OF MY POTENTIAL.

The most successful and fulfilled people in the world have one thing in common. They push themselves to the edge of their potential. You have unlimited potential inside of you. Listen to your heart. It will show you the way forward to reach your full purpose. Now is a great time to set goals and work toward them. With actionable goals, you set yourself up for success by having a road map to follow. Your potential is in the goals and dreams you hold in your heart. By following your heart and doing what you love, your anxieties will fade.

◇ ◇ ◇ ◇

I am living my dream life. I am always aligned with my truth, which is an expression of love. I choose to see my life as a creative adventure, one in which I explore my full potential. I live on the edge of my own creativity and push forward into new possibilities.

◇ ◇ ◇ ◇

What new possibilities can I create for myself?

MY LIFE IS AN EXPERIMENT.
I EMBRACE THE EXPLORATION.

It's easy to get caught up in the cycle of work and play and exist rather than actually live your life. In the hustle and bustle of trying to survive, we often forget that we were meant for more than just a mundane existence. Life should be a boundless exploration, so dive into your life as if it were a giant exploration and epic journey. Approach life as an experiment you get to create, try, and retry. The scientific method is a series of trial-and-error experiments that play out until the desired results are achieved. When you go for what you want and it doesn't work out the way you hoped, it's not a failure or a mistake; it's simply part of the process of exploration.

Embrace your life as if it were trial and error. You get to try things and see what works and what doesn't. When you look at your life as an experiment, you will be less burdened by external situations.

◇ ◇ ◇ ◇

I live my life fully by setting intentions and exploring new ways of being. I connect with my divine truth, which shows me the next action step to take. I explore my life as if it were a creative adventure. I am on an epic journey to live from my heart. I enjoy trying new things and seeing new outcomes.

◇ ◇ ◇ ◇

What experiment am I currently trying?

I SMILE AT STRANGERS.

The simple act of smiling can make you feel better. When you smile, the feel-good neurotransmitter dopamine is released. This helps you feel more relaxed and happy. Smiling is a form of kindness. Not only does it help you feel better, but it makes you more approachable.

Smiling at other people builds a connection and helps establish rapport. Step out of your comfort zone by making eye contact and smiling at strangers. You may surprise yourself and make a new connection. Strangers are just friends you have yet to meet, and a smile can bridge that gap.

◇ ◇ ◇ ◇

I smile confidently and with great love. I look at others and welcome them into my life. I am connected to my best self, who is happy, healthy, and open to meeting others. When I smile at strangers, they feel warm and respected. I am happy to share smiles with those I love. We are all connected, and a smile brings us closer.

◇ ◇ ◇ ◇

How has my smile helped me get close to others?

ALL NEW THINGS REQUIRE DISCOMFORT.

When you embark on a self-improvement path, you may grow uncomfortable. New habits create new results, but this produces a new way of being. When you desire something, you have to become the person who can receive that desire. This is why there is a universal buffer between what you want and where you currently stand.

You have to learn, grow, change, and become more of the person you truly want to be. This is a natural part of life but one that will require you to be uncomfortable. All new stages of our life require discomfort. Learning how to be comfortable when you are uncomfortable is the key to success.

◇ ◇ ◇ ◇

I am open to change. I am growing more into the person I want to become. I am comfortable with the uncomfortable aspect of growth. I know that all greatness requires a transition period, and I navigate mine gracefully. I grow with dedication and commitment to becoming more of who I really am.

◇ ◇ ◇ ◇

What recent change has caused me to be uncomfortable?

I SET FUN AND RECREATION GOALS.

You may feel the need for more balance in your life. If you are stressed out or overwhelmed with particular demands, it is essential to carve out more you time. One successful strategy is to actually schedule fun time into your schedule. Playtime is essential for your happiness and productivity, but setting goals in this arena will boost your happiness tenfold.

Create a big-picture view of your life and think about what is most important to you when it comes to having more fun. Have you always wanted to explore a nearby city or try a new hobby? Set fun goals for yourself and watch yourself become more balanced.

◇ ◇ ◇ ◇

I set goals that are fun and actionable. I create time for me and carve out space to play. When I add more play into my life, I am connected to my true self and I am balanced.

◇ ◇ ◇ ◇

What fun goal can I set for myself?

Day 276

NATURE IS MY SANCTUARY.

If you are feeling frustrated, overwhelmed, stressed, or angry, return to your natural state, one that is in harmony with the world. Going into nature will help calm your body and mind. Nature has no anger. It is patient, and nature is kind. There is a natural flow and understanding to all things in nature.

The tree does not yell at itself, "Hurry up and grow!" It takes its time, and patience is its virtue. The same goes for grass that grows toward the sunlight. It reaches for fresh air. Nature can be your greatest teacher to help you return to self and learn valuable life lessons.

◇ ◇ ◇ ◇

When I become anxious, I return to my true self, which is in harmony with the world. I am balanced because I seek sanctuary in nature. Being in nature helps me heal my worries and return to happiness.

◇ ◇ ◇ ◇

How can I bring more nature into my life?

I AM A HEALER.

You have great healing capacity inside of you. You may feel rundown or troubled by sickness in yourself or others, but this does not need to stop you from shining your authentic light. Focus on your healing capabilities with love and compassion. You may be sensitive to the needs of those closest to you. You can help them by being there for them. Often, behind smiles there is pain. You can become the restorer of happiness by holding space for others.

You don't need to judge or try to fix anyone, just be with them. You are a vessel of light and love, and by sharing this with others, you heal yourself and the world. Too often, you become fixated on your own situations. Today is a reminder that you can encourage the discouraged. Don't wait for a miracle. Become the miracle.

◇ ◇ ◇ ◇

I can heal the world. I lift up those who are down with my encouragement and love. I am compassionate in all of my endeavors and interactions. I see light where there is darkness. I see hope where there hopelessness. I see love in the face of fear. I am a healer and a light worker. I have the capacity to change the world by focusing on love.

◇ ◇ ◇ ◇

How can I embrace my characteristics as a healer?

ALL DISEASE AND DISCOMFORT ARE MANIFESTATIONS OF A THOUGHT PATTERN IN MY MIND.

Your thoughts are an integral part of your expression of life. What you think, you become. When you feel out of alignment or not balanced, return to your thoughts and focus on holding positive energy. The disease in your body is a manifestation of thoughts from your previous path.

If you hold on to negative patterns, they will form into outward expressions. Release all fear-based thoughts and cleanse yourself regularly. You can clear yourself with white light and with the meditation below.

◇ ◇ ◇ ◇

I create loving expressions of my truth. My body is in perfect health. Any disease I experience is an opportunity for me to learn more about myself.

I choose healthy habits for my body and life. I move in a way that helps serve my greatest good. I focus on what is essential for me to move forward, and I embody my sprit as I create healthy habits. I release all fear-based thoughts and attach myself to positive energy. I am free of physical pain and worry. I am centered in my truth.

◇ ◇ ◇ ◇

Where can I be more true to myself and align
with positive intentions?

I REALIGN WITH MY DESIRES DAILY.

It is okay to refresh yourself and take steps to cultivate new habits. Today is about being more vulnerable with yourself. Look at your identity and who you are. Discern what is important to you. Certain relationships and situations in your life might be blocking you from reaching your goals. It is important for you to realign with your goals daily.

You are always changing and growing. Becoming more of who you are is a process that comes with new desires. Allow yourself to assess and recalibrate your goals to make sure you are aligned with your truth.

◇ ◇ ◇ ◇

I am connected to my highest vibration and truth. When I focus forward, I leave no room for error because my heart is in the driver's seat of my life. I am aligned with my soul's purpose and true desires. I reevaluate often to ensure I am aligned with my highest good. All my desires are manifesting with love, and I am comfortable in the process.

◇ ◇ ◇ ◇

What desire do I need to revisit?

Day 280

I CHOOSE MY WORDS WISELY.

Expressing yourself through language is a gift. The words you choose have a powerful impact on your overall outcome. When you choose words like "hate," you are sending out negative energy. What you resist will always persist. Make a conscious effort not to say words that shed evil energy. Find a better way to release anger. Your words are powerful expressions of your truth. Use your words wisely.

◇ ◇ ◇ ◇

I choose my words with conscious focus and energy. I do not use unnecessary words to get my point across. All of my vocabulary is part of my essence and how I project myself into the world. I choose positive words that are uplifting and energetically light. I do not send hateful words out into the world. I reach out to my enemies with love and kindness. My words are my greatest expressions of self.

◇ ◇ ◇ ◇

What words can I eliminate from my vocabulary?

I ACTIVELY LIVE MY HIGHEST AWARENESS.

You are always changing, growing, and morphing into more of who you really are. You are not the same person you were when you woke up this morning, nor are you the same person as you were a year ago. Let yourself grow and change as you learn more and expand your consciousness. Holding on to old beliefs out of habit will not serve you. It is time to spread your wings and let yourself fly.

◇ ◇ ◇ ◇

I am changing. I am growing. All my senses come to life as I morph into the new me that awaits. The Universe is guiding me to new beginnings as I cocreate with my highest good. I live from integrity, and I live out my truth. I trust what I know, and my new awareness leads me to happiness and true health.

◇ ◇ ◇ ◇

What new beginning am I being guided to?

I DO NOT BUY INTO OTHER PEOPLE'S EVALUATIONS OF ME.

What people say to you or about you is not fact. You don't have to accept their evaluations. You can believe them or you can believe in yourself. The only thing that matters is how you see yourself. People will always have a point of view, but your only mission is to evaluate yourself based on love and compassion. You can never judge a person's life or understand what they are going through. Let others have their opinions, but pay no attention to them.

◇ ◇ ◇ ◇

I am happy to be me. I am comfortable with myself and pay no attention to what others say or think about me. When I am proud of myself and my accomplishments, I don't need the approval of others. I do not buy into other people's evaluations of me. I only care about what I think about myself.

◇ ◇ ◇ ◇

What hurtful thing did someone say about me that
I can let go of?

EVERYONE IS ON THEIR OWN JOURNEY.

Comparing yourself to others is hurting you. You feel either inferior or superior, but neither is the truth. Everyone is equal, and you are your own unique person. You are a unique, wonderful spirit with beautiful gifts to give to the world. There is no one to compare yourself to because everyone is unique and on their own journey.

Everything in the physical world is part of transition and change. Comparing yourself to others is a waste of time because everything is always changing. Allow yourself to flow with changes and turn inward. Your true essence is your internal being. Your spirit is deeper and realer than any external body or change.

◇ ◇ ◇ ◇

I love myself and other people unconditionally. I am unique and one of a kind. There is no other person who has ever been like me, and I celebrate my oneness. There is nothing to compare, for I am on my own journey and I am true to myself.

◇ ◇ ◇ ◇

Who do I keep comparing myself to?
I release my need to be like others. I am my own unique self.

Day 284

I EXPLORE MY FEARS, SO I CAN RELEASE THEM FOR GOOD.

Fear is not bad. Fear is connected to your ego, and your ego just wants to protect you. Instead of running from your fear, give it love. Fear is like a lonely child looking for attention. It will lash out to be heard and seen, but you don't have to let it control your life. If you look at your fear the same way you would a young child, you will see that it just needs attention. When you can see the truth behind your fear, it will no longer try to control you.

Resistance is outwardly experienced as fear. The amount of fear is equivalent to the degree of resistance, which means the more fear you feel about a situation, the more certain you should be that the venture is important to the growth of your soul. If it meant nothing to you, you would feel no resistance. Resistance shows up to ask us to look deep into our hearts to see what we care most about.

◇ ◇ ◇ ◇

I am detached from the outcome. I am not afraid of my fear, for it is trying to guide me back to safety. I look at my fear and see what it is trying to tell me. The more fear I feel, the more attention that area of my life needs. Usually fear is an indicator of what I care about the most.

◇ ◇ ◇ ◇

My fear is good. It is a compass into areas of growth. The more scared I am, the surer I am that I have to go for it.

THE UNIVERSE IS TESTING ME.

Your life is a master plan of seasons inspired by your soul. You may have a dream you are working toward. The Universe will test you. Areas of your life need more awareness, and the Universe will bring people, places, and situations to you to help you overcome the challenges and learn the lessons.

You may ask the Universe or pray for love. Trust you will always get what you ask for, but it might be in a different form. The Universe may bring you unloving or unkind people. This is for you to practice what you desire. If you want to be more loving and committed to kindness, then practice it in the face of adversity. Everything is always changing, but your heart does not waver. What you desire is on its way to you, but you must be present to the universal lessons.

$$\diamond \ \diamond \ \diamond \ \diamond$$

My power comes through my mind and my connection to my heart. The Universe will test me, but I am always up for the challenge. I see opportunity in the expansive nature of being true to myself. I seek out what I desire and practice my values daily. I will attract what I want when I become what I want.

$$\diamond \ \diamond \ \diamond \ \diamond$$

How is the Universe testing me?

I ASK FOR FEEDBACK.

You may be in a relationship or situation and feel unsure of where it is going. If you are going along and feel stuck in the motions of life, look at your communication. Having a communication plan with others will help you feel more purposeful and connected. In romantic relationships or work environments, opening yourself up to feedback will help you assess your overall plan. Be open to receiving information from others. Ask for feedback about your relationship, your process, and your own growth. Listening to others will help you reevaluate and grow.

◇ ◇ ◇ ◇

I am open to hearing from others and listening to their honest feedback. I want to improve my life and my communication with others. Feedback is essential for my growth and development. I take what works and leave what doesn't. Feedback is a communication tool that helps me connect with those I care about.

◇ ◇ ◇ ◇

What relationship can I ask for feedback in?

I GET OUT OF THE "BUT" ZONE.

Look at a current situation that is causing you the most stress and see if you are making excuses. Are you blaming others or wondering why it hasn't happened yet? Maybe you are focusing on what you want, but you keep falling into the "but" zone. The "but" zone is where you say, "I want to lose weight, *but* I am too tired to exercise." "I want to find a soul mate, *but* no one approaches me." Focus back on your intentions and align with your desires. Leave the buts out of the equation and watch what you want come to you faster.

◇ ◇ ◇ ◇

I refuse to make excuses for my circumstances. I am accountable and connected to my desires. What I experience is a direct reflection of what I have been thinking about. I know I don't have control over some things in my life, but I have control over my thoughts about my life. I can choose to focus on expansive opportunities, and I stay out of the "but" zone.

◇ ◇ ◇ ◇

What excuses will I kick to the curb?

CONTINUOUS EFFORT GIVES ME UNLIMITED POTENTIAL.

You might be feeling down and out. You have been focusing more attention on what isn't working than what is. When you are on a path of self-improvement, it is the steps along the way that make the big path possible.

Stop focusing so much on what isn't working and put your energy into potential. No matter what, keep going. Do not give up. When the dream is in your heart, persistence is essential. It may take time to manifest, but when you hold the intention of why you want what you want, it will come true. Forget a timeline and just keep going.

◇ ◇ ◇ ◇

I release my need to manifest the outcome, and I trust divine timing. I am fully in the process of my life. I keep going and try new things. I know my dreams come true with continued focus and attention. I put forth all of my attention and live my unlimited potential.

◇ ◇ ◇ ◇

What dream can I keep giving attention?

I DON'T HAVE TO SEE THE WHOLE PATH. I TAKE ONE STEP AT A TIME.

Are you overwhelmed by the burden of the tasks in front of you? Your goals require action, and when you get inspired, you should take steps forward. You don't have to know which action. There is no wrong action, as long as you are taking action forward.

You may be focusing too much on the end destination. Rewind your attention by focusing more on what you can do in this moment. One step at a time will give you the results your truly desire. Keep moving forward.

◇ ◇ ◇ ◇

I trust my future, and my plans are unfolding perfectly. I don't have to see the entire path. I just take one step at a time. Each step I take reveals the next best step forward. I am connected to my life's purpose by taking action and trusting the guidance I receive.

◇ ◇ ◇ ◇

What one step can I take to help me get to my goal?

I AM CLEAR WITH MY INTENTIONS.

The clearer you are with what you desire, the easier your manifestation process will be. If you are going back and forth on what you want, the Universe will waver as well. Get clear with your intentions and focus forward with energetic enthusiasm. When you hold the belief that your dreams are coming true, and you do not waver, the manifestation will happen rapidly. Be clear with why you want what you want and do not back down on your dreams.

◇ ◇ ◇ ◇

I do not let fear stop me. I focus on what I want and keep my attention focused on my desire. I am dedicated to my dreams, and I align my actions to match my goals. Everything I do is focused on me receiving my goals. I am purposeful in my interactions and clear with my intentions.

◇ ◇ ◇ ◇

What goal of mine needs more clarity?

MY FINANCIAL ABUNDANCE IS REFLECTED IN WHAT I SEE.

A limited belief or thought that may be holding you back is the belief that there are not enough resources, time, or money to go around. If you feel trapped by life's circumstances, look to the beliefs you have been carrying around about the situation. When you see others in abundance and prosperity, see it as a mirror of your own abundance and what is on its way to you. There is no need to feel a lack mentality or as though there is not enough for everyone. You are connected to your abundance when you focus on your worth.

◇ ◇ ◇ ◇

My thoughts determine my own prosperity. I am worth what I think I am worth. I am grateful for what I have, for it increases my abundance and wealth. I recognize financial abundance in every experience and welcome it to me. I am abundant and secure.

◇ ◇ ◇ ◇

What outward expression of wealth do I keep seeing?
How is this a reflection of my own desires?

Day 292

I DETACH FROM SOCIAL VAMPIRES.

Look at all of your relationships and see who is bringing you down. Some people like to talk about their dramas, their insecurities, and their fears. This energy can be draining and keep you from focusing on your best self. Disengage from negative people and detach from those relationships. When you do this, you will align with your own best self and feel more grounded.

Your positivity is important right now. Releasing friends who no longer serve you creates space to welcome in new, more optimistic friends. Surround yourself with positive and supportive people.

◇ ◇ ◇ ◇

I let go of all demeaning relationships. I release my attachment to old friends who cause me frustration and stress. I surround myself with kind, loving, and supportive people. Together we accomplish great things because my support system is solid and full of positive energy and light.

◇ ◇ ◇ ◇

What relationship causes me the most emotional stress? What steps can I take to release this person from my life?

Day 293

I SEE THE REWARD IN TAKING RISKS.

All great outcomes involve great risk. Most risk involved is emotional, like in stepping out of your comfort zone and doing what you haven't done before. Assess your current comfort zone and see where you are playing it safe. Think about your core desire and what you want.

As you use this as your target to move forward, you will see the power of taking great risks. All risk has reward. You will gain valuable experiences and grow into who you are meant to be. Give yourself permission to go for it and try new experiments. To get the results you want, you will need to take greater risks.

◇ ◇ ◇ ◇

I take risks with love and dedication to my greater good. I know what I want and I take steps to get there. All great challenges are overcome by taking risks. My reward is in the journey of life as I take more chances and grow. I invite new risk into my life, for the reward will be gratifying.

◇ ◇ ◇ ◇

What risk can I take to help reach my goal?

I CREATE MY FUTURE BY ENVISIONING IT.

When you visualize what you want, you give the Universe an opportunity to filter in resources to help you get it. You will only see enough to match your vision. So be careful to not limit yourself. Instead, expand your mind by removing limiting beliefs and negative thoughts. By visualizing your success, you will reach your goals faster. You have to believe it and see it before you can receive it.

◇ ◇ ◇ ◇

I hold the vision of what I want. I do not spend time focusing on any negative thoughts or limiting beliefs. Every action I take keeps me on track to live my big-picture plan. I create my ideal life by envisioning it every day.

◇ ◇ ◇ ◇

What limiting belief is blocking me from creating my ideal future?

I ALLOW MYSELF TO JUST
BE WHO I AM.

Love yourself in this very moment. As you are, no pretenses, no forced interactions. There is nothing for you to say and do. There is nothing for you to be. Accept who you are. If you believe you have to wait to accept yourself, when you lose weight or grow your hair out, or get the job or the relationship, or finally receive the financial support, you are keeping yourself on the outside looking in on your own life. Self-acceptance comes from within. It does not come from the experiences outside of yourself. Drop your list of expectations and see how beautiful and awesome you really are.

◇ ◇ ◇ ◇

I no longer resist accepting myself, for I am an expression of love. I enjoy showing the world who I really am. I am love. I drop my list of expectations and accept myself as I am. I allow myself to be who I really am.

◇ ◇ ◇ ◇

What part of myself have I been unwilling to accept?

EVERYONE IS FAMILY.

You have your close family, and you are surrounded by love, but all living beings are part of your family. Looking at strangers as outsiders hurts your ability to feel connected and appreciated. Everyone you have ever met and come in contact with is part of an intricate web of universal souls connected to divine love. This unconditional love connects us all. When you refuse to forgive, you are hurting your family and, therefore, hurting yourself. When you look only at your family's limitations, you fail to see the opportunities of compassion. Look at everyone as if they were part of your true family, and you will feel more aligned with real love.

◇ ◇ ◇ ◇

I choose my family. I have the perfect family for me to learn what I need to learn. My parents have given me valuable lessons in love, self-acceptance, forgiveness, and loyalty. I let go of all limiting beliefs that separate me from others. Everyone in my life is part of a beautiful unconditional support system. We are all family. We are one.

◇ ◇ ◇ ◇

What family member do I need to forgive?

Day 297

I AM AWARE OF MY STORIES.

The limitations in your life are primarily caused by the stories in your mind. You have experiences from your past that have resulted in reactions, which create stories. The stories are illusions that separate you from the truth. Look deep into your heart to see the truth.

That person you think dislikes you is really just trying to make it through their own life. It has nothing to do with you. That comment your significant other made has nothing to do with you. The stories you create keep you playing small and prevent you from living to your full potential. Become aware of the message your stories are trying to tell you and release them for good.

◇ ◇ ◇ ◇

I am honest with myself and see situations, as they are, not how I wish them to be. I do not lean on false fabrications of reality or on illusions. I turn to the truth and see thing as they are. I take emotion out of situations, so I can be connected to the truth and have an unbiased approach. I am aware of my stories, and I transform them with love.

◇ ◇ ◇ ◇

What story is preventing me from seeing my true greatness?

I BEHAVE MY WAY TO SUCCESS.

You may have goals and desired outcomes, but your current habits might not be aligned with the results you truly desire. If you want to be fit, but you currently overeat and don't exercise, you are at a contrast from your true outcome.

Instead of focusing on self-doubt or criticizing yourself for not being able to reach your goals, look closely at your current habits. Examine your behaviors and clear up your routine. Become the person you need to be to reach success. Start to behave your way to your desired outcome.

◇ ◇ ◇ ◇

My habits are aligned with my desired outcome. I am vibrating my dreams by being what I want to achieve. I focus my energy into my behavior, acting my way to success.

◇ ◇ ◇ ◇

What behavior do I have that contradicts my desired outcome?

Day 299

I TAKE TIME TO GRIEVE.

The passing of a loved one or losing a person or pet in your life through transition, death, or disease can be troubling. Give yourself time and space to go through the natural process of losing aspects of life. Be gentle and compassionate with yourself, for grieving is a process. There is no expiration date on a healed heart.

Only time will give you what you need. If you have lost a loved one, know they are never gone. They will live in your heart forever, and their spirit is always with you. Believe you will connect with their soul again, and all is truly well.

◇ ◇ ◇ ◇

I am at peace with all of life. I allow myself to heal in the natural process of losing a loved one. I grieve the lost love, but they are in my heart forever. I smile when I think of them, for they are always with me in spirit, and with love I send them light.

◇ ◇ ◇ ◇

How can I be more compassionate with myself through the grieving process?

I GO FOR IT.

Do not stop yourself because of fear or limiting beliefs. Just because it hasn't been done doesn't mean it's not for you to do. Go for it and give it all you've got. If the goal is in your heart and the inspiration strikes, it is time for you to take action.

There may be an area of your life in which you are holding yourself back. This is a reminder to let go of all external distractions and just dive in. Go for it and persevere.

◇ ◇ ◇ ◇

I stop making excuses, and I jump in fully to the experiment of my life. I go for it and give it all I have. I tell the Universe my desire and focus fully on receiving the outcome. I live my full purpose by acting out my goals. I go for it by taking action and trying new things. I do not allow any distractions. I am focused and determined, and I will succeed.

◇ ◇ ◇ ◇

What does my heart want me to go for?

I BELONG HERE.

You have worked really hard to get where you are. You may feel ready to step into the next phase of your life, but sometimes your insecurities step in the way. Your ego may be trying to keep you from feeling your greatness; it may say things like you aren't enough, you messed up, you aren't doing a good job. This is your fear, and it is not based on the truth. The truth is you are love and light, and you are needed here. Where you are today is important because it is part of you living your potential. Don't shy away from your greatness. Instead, see yourself the way others do: special, important, and needed.

◇ ◇ ◇ ◇

I have special gifts, talents, opinions, and reasons for being here. I matter, and I am important. I belong here and am exactly where I need to be. Everything I have ever done has prepared me for this moment, and today I stand proud to be here because I know I belong. The world needs my light and me.

◇ ◇ ◇ ◇

What special skills, talents, and perspectives make me unique?

"

I Do Not
Judge Myself
for Feeling My
Feelings.

"

Day 302

I DO NOT JUDGE MYSELF FOR FEELING MY FEELINGS.

Check in with yourself and see if you are judging yourself for feeling your feelings. So many people feel guilty for feeling angry because they can't feel happy. When you judge yourself for your emotions, you keep yourself in the vicious cycle of self-doubt and denial. Express your feelings as much as you can. Allow yourself to cry, scream in the car, or share your sadness with a significant other. Expressing your feelings means expressing your true nature. Don't deny yourself expressions of life.

◇ ◇ ◇ ◇

I allow myself to feel my feelings. I do not judge myself or put limitations on how I feel. Each emotion is an energy that needs to be released. My feelings are all thoughts that vibrate in my body, and I create my own healing by feeling my feelings. My honest expression of self is shared through my emotions.

◇ ◇ ◇ ◇

How do I judge myself for certain feelings I feel?

ONE DAY AT A TIME.

It's easy to get caught up in what you could have done yesterday or what you plan to do tomorrow, but less easy to keep yourself in the here and now. When you do this, you miss opportunities for greatness and trap yourself in a cycle of never-changing habits. It is time to let go of yesterday and quit dwelling on tomorrow. Your previous or future actions and results have no bearing on today. Each day when you wake, you have a new opportunity to start over. If you are trying to break a habit or an addiction, compassion and love will lead the way. There is no need to overthink your previous behaviors. Instead, empower yourself by focusing on healthy actions you can take today. One day at a time will help bring you to health.

◇ ◇ ◇ ◇

I let go of my old habits and negative thought patterns. I am connected to my desire, and I make healthy choices aligned with my goal. I forgive myself for pain I have caused my body. My spirit knows great learning is in my addictions and self-sabotaging habits. Instead of self-hate, I turn to love and compassion. My heart will guide the way to happiness and health.

◇ ◇ ◇ ◇

What self-sabotaging habit can I forgive myself for?

Day 304

I NOURISH MY NUDGES.

Inspiration comes to you all the time. Is there some notion tapping at the back door of your mind just waiting for you to notice it? When you get a new idea or a desire strikes your heart, it is time to nourish that nudge. Your dreams can only manifest when you take action, even if it's slow forward movement to start with. A nudge can take you from a small step to a big leap. Pay attention to the outcome you want to receive and focus on action steps to help you get there.

◇ ◇ ◇ ◇

I pay attention to my heart's desires. When inspiration strikes my heart, I take action immediately. There is no need to hesitate. The path will be revealed as I take action and step forward.

◇ ◇ ◇ ◇

What nudge have I been receiving that I can nourish?

EVERYTHING ISN'T HAPPENING TO ME. IT'S HAPPENING FOR ME.

Right now it may seem like everything that could is going wrong. Consider that things don't happen to you but for you. What if everything in your life right now will help you get to where your soul wants to be? Instead of resisting what is, accept it. The Universe will never give you what you can't handle. Even if it looks like the Universe is out to destroy your plans, it could be guiding you closer to what your heart truly desires in the grand scheme of things. Always trust the process.

Everything in your life is part of a carefully constructed plan, created just for you, by you. The Universe is in collaboration with you and your dreams. Imagine your life is not a series of events outside of yourself but a created action plan devised by you and the Universe.

When you see the situations in your life as part of a universal plan, you will feel less burdened. If something didn't go as planned, instead of looking at the situation as a curse or setback, see it as a blessing or an opportunity.

◇ ◇ ◇ ◇

I am always right where I need to be. My life is unfolding perfectly according to the plan I created with the Universe. If there is anything I dislike, I remove it with love. The situations in my life don't happen to me, they happen for me.

◇ ◇ ◇ ◇

What situation is happening for me instead of to me?

I AVOID EMOTIONAL REASONING.

Don't believe that what you feel is actually true. Your feelings are a guidance system, but be careful not to assume they are facts. You may be thinking your feelings are the truth, but this prevents you from seeing the honest picture of life. For example, if you feel rejected because someone turned you down, that doesn't mean you are unlovable or unworthy of other people's time. But if you believe your emotions and let them reason for you, you could block yourself from feeling confident.

◇ ◇ ◇ ◇

I do not assume anything or pretend to know what others are thinking and feeling. I attune with my true desires and feel my feelings without attaching emotion to them. I am logical with my evaluations of situations by removing my fears and feelings. I don't take things personally. I avoid emotional reasoning.

◇ ◇ ◇ ◇

How has emotional reasoning clouded my point of view?

MY CHOICES ARE NOT FOREVER OR FINAL.

Every choice you make is a brilliant exploration of yourself. You have an opportunity to align with your desires and learn what doesn't work for you. When you are stuck trying to make a choice, ask yourself if you are worried about the outcome. Most of the time, people fail to move forward because they think their choice will be a final move.

Nothing is ever final or finished. The job you take, the relationship you enter, and the home you live in are all temporary choices. Some choices last a few days, some decades. The time is irrelevant when it comes to making the choice. Just choose what feels right for you in the moment.

◇ ◇ ◇ ◇

I make choices from a love-filled place. I do not overthink my choices. I do what feels right. I embrace the journey of my life and trust that things are unfolding as they are supposed to. Every choice I make is part of a greater understanding of myself. I make choices with love, and I am confident in the direction I am going.

◇ ◇ ◇ ◇

What choice have I been afraid to make?

I ASK WHAT LESSON I CAN LEARN.

Every situation you are in is an opportunity for you to learn. If a situation keeps repeating itself, ask, "Why am I here? What can I learn?" You will receive guidance as to the lesson available for you. Instead of resisting or trying to power your way through the problem, let love guide you. The Universe will support you in moving to clarity, but you must ask for help.

◇ ◇ ◇ ◇

I am never stuck. I am not a victim of my own life's circumstances. I choose to embrace the journey of life with a focus on growth. I am always learning. If I don't know why I am in a situation, I ask what can I learn. The answer is always revealed to me.

◇ ◇ ◇ ◇

What lesson can I learn from a troubling situation?

Day 309

AM I FAILING ENOUGH?

Thomas Edison said it best: "I have not failed. I've just found ten thousand ways that won't work." But with a little more perseverance, electricity was born. Never give up on your dreams. Keep going. With each new failure, you have an opportunity to achieve success.

If you aren't failing enough, you aren't trying hard enough. You may be afraid of failing, but the greatest failures lead to the greatest rewards. In order to live a passionate, purpose-filled life, take more risks and don't be afraid to fail.

◇ ◇ ◇ ◇

I am open to taking risks. I am not afraid of failing, for all failures lead me to the truth. There is no such thing as failure because I grow each time. I learn more about myself through the process of trying new things. I embrace the opportunity to grow as a person by exploring life's contrasts. I give myself permission to fail.

◇ ◇ ◇ ◇

How can I fail harder?

I GAUGE MY HAPPINESS BY HOW MUCH FUN I AM HAVING.

Happy people gauge their happiness by the amount of fun they're having. Happy people absolutely love their jobs. For many, it doesn't feel like they work a day of their lives, in fact. It's mostly play. How can you add more play into your day? When you make having fun a priority, everything feels more enjoyable. If you want to be happy beyond your wildest dreams, ask yourself if you're having fun.

◇ ◇ ◇ ◇

I choose to play my way to happiness. When I add more fun into my life, I am happy and fulfilled. I choose work, relationships, foods, and places that bring me joy. I am always having fun, for it is my number one priority.

◇ ◇ ◇ ◇

How can I add more fun into my life?

Day 311

I EXPECT GREAT RESULTS.

Expect great things for yourself. You've done a great deal of work, and now it is time to step back and let the situation just be. Refocus your energy by expecting the best outcome possible. Your actions can manifest into your desires in endless ways. Let go of how it happens, and just know it will. You are in control of your outcome. Keep focusing on the results you want. Expect great things for yourself. And don't give up. Today is a time to look inward and be honest. Where have you been settling? Now is the time to raise your standards.

◇ ◇ ◇ ◇

I feel good about my actions and all that I do. I flow through life with effortless ease. I have high expectations and do not settle. My life is part of an ever-expansive journey. I relax into the rhyme of the process by being in the journey. I expect great things for myself and those around me. I know my intentions and actions will manifest, and I will get what I want.

◇ ◇ ◇ ◇

Where can I raise my expectations?

I AM SUCCEEDING AT LIFE.

No matter how hard your life feels right now, consider how far you've already come. When you were young, you may have felt invincible, as though you could conquer the world. Your idealistic approach to life gave you the badge of courage that was needed to ignore difficulties. But one life stress after another can pile on and tear down that courageous wall, leaving resentment, regret, and fear.

Return to your childlike heroic self and recognize how great you are doing. When you can visit your younger self, he or she will tell you there's no need to worry because everything always works out in the end. For today, hang up your concerns and celebrate how well you are doing at life.

◇ ◇ ◇ ◇

My life is an adventure full of exploration and awe. The situations that cause me the most anxiety today will soon fade away. I am not connected to the outcome, for I focus on what I want and expect it to come to me. I know I am doing a great job at life.

◇ ◇ ◇ ◇

What childlike sense of wonder can I bring into my adult life?

I AM NOT MY PROBLEMS.

Do you identify with your problems like the skin on your body? Your problems are not part of you. Allow them to come and go and don't identify with them. Instead of focusing on your problems, be led by the desires in your heart. The more you focus on what you want, the less of what you don't want will show up.

◇ ◇ ◇ ◇

I take all my attention off of my dislikes and focus solely on my likes. I see the good in all situations, and the possibilities are endless. My problems are not problems at all but areas of my life that need more love. I focus on my insecurities and troubling situations with love and send light to each situation.

◇ ◇ ◇ ◇

What problem do I spend most of my attention on?
I send it love.

Day 314

I DON'T HAVE TO BE HAPPY
ALL THE TIME.

On any given day, the average person will have more than fifty thousand thoughts. Of these, more than 80 percent can be negative. Most of these thoughts are self-deprecating. Pay attention to your thoughts and see if you are mad at yourself for not being happier. You may feel guilty because you aren't where you think you should be. Turn your negative thoughts into more loving thoughts by consciously focusing on your energy. When you are aware of your thoughts, you can control them.

◇ ◇ ◇ ◇

I am perfectly content with where I am in this moment. I am present in my life, and I feel my feelings. Every moment is a new opportunity to feel my emotions and let them work through me. I am connected to my life by being present and open to new opportunities. I remove all self-sabotaging thoughts and negativity by focusing on love.

◇ ◇ ◇ ◇

How can I stop getting mad at myself for not being happier?

Day 315

I BELONG.

No two people are created the same. These huge differences can make us feel alone and left out. If you struggle to feel as though you belong, know you are not alone. Every other person on the planet feels the same way, which makes us united in our differences. Embrace your unique self. The world needs you as you are.

◇ ◇ ◇ ◇

I embrace my authentic self. I know I am different, and that makes me beautiful. I don't try to fit in because I am supposed to stand out. I celebrate my unique self. I belong.

◇ ◇ ◇ ◇

What difference about me is a unique gift?

WHEN I AM CONFIDENT, NEGATIVITY CAN'T GET ME DOWN.

Haters seem to spring up when you try to do a great job: a critic of your parenting skills, your relationship status (or lack thereof), how you dress, where you live, or your weight. At the end of all the haters' catcalls is an invitation to low self-esteem and self-loathing. Don't listen to the negativity.

Are negative people affecting your actions? Has someone recently attacked you for something you did? Or does the idea of someone lashing out prevent you from acting? Ask yourself if you're actually allowing what people could say to stop you from following your own heart. Recognize that haters can't get to you when you feel confident and self-assured. The best way to avoid feeling victimized by the string of negativity is to improve your relationship with yourself.

◇ ◇ ◇ ◇

I am not what other people say I am. I am confident and secure with my own self. I don't waste time on haters or their focus on my habits. I align with my highest good and surround myself with love and light. I am confident in my skin and proud of who I am.

◇ ◇ ◇ ◇

When do I feel the most confident?

Day 317

MY BODY KNOWS HOW TO HEAL ITSELF. MY ONLY JOB IS TO GET OUT OF ITS WAY.

Your body is working hard to maintain its health. You may be criticizing yourself by attacking your body with negative thoughts, or over-stuffing it with extra food. Treat your body as a friend by showing it love and compassion. Your body is not the enemy. In fact, your body has a healing message for you. It knows how to heal itself. You just have to listen to its wisdom.

◇ ◇ ◇ ◇

My body is my greatest tool for health. I return to wellness by sending love to my body. I trust the divine timing of my healing, and I let my body be the teacher. I listen to my body and give it what it needs.

◇ ◇ ◇ ◇

My body is my greatest teacher.
What message does it have for me?

I LIVE FOR THE MOMENT.

You might be working too hard to reach a particular outcome. It is good to have things to look forward to, but this moment is where life is happening. Live for this moment by being present. The greatest gift you can give yourself is to focus on the now. Stop worrying about the pain from yesterday or your what-ifs about tomorrow. Instead, be here now.

◇ ◇ ◇ ◇

I am still here now. I am present. All I have ever done has led me to right now. I am comfortable with who I am in this moment. I forgive myself for past burdens. It was all part of my journey. For today, things are as they should be. I embrace this moment for all eternity.

◇ ◇ ◇ ◇

What life am I missing today by reaching for tomorrow?

I MAKE HAPPINESS MY FAVORITE HABIT.

Happiness is linked to your inner desire to feel connected and loved. When you're happy, you feel confident, purposeful, and in harmony with your true self. People who are genuinely happy are healthier and kinder and have better relationships. Truly happy people don't try to get happy. They just are happy because they recognize the magic of happiness is in the moment. You can train your brain to see the good in every situation and make happiness a habit.

◇ ◇ ◇ ◇

I make happiness my favorite habit. I know I can choose to be in love or fear. Happiness is a love vibration that pulses through my body. I make healthy choices that make me feel good. I don't attack myself with criticism or negative energy. I love my life and myself. Happiness is my guiding source of inspiration.

◇ ◇ ◇ ◇

What habit needs a happiness boost?

THE SECRET TO HAVING IT ALL IS BEING THANKFUL FOR IT ALL.

Gratitude is the life force of everything. You might be focusing too much on what you don't have. If you are comparing yourself to others and observing what they have in relation to you, realize this is a mirror to your own potential. If someone seems thinner, smarter, and prettier, or has what you want, see this as a reflection of what is possible for you. Jealousy is a lack of love in an area of your life you desire most. If you want to have it all, be thankful for what you already have.

◇ ◇ ◇ ◇

I am thankful for everything in my life. Even my insecurities are an opportunity for more self-awareness and compassion. I see all challenges as divine opportunities for growth. I look at my life as a creative adventure and see the results of my positive thinking. I focus on what I want and am thankful for all I have.

◇ ◇ ◇ ◇

What insecurity can I be thankful for?

I FOCUS ON RESULTS, NOT REASONS.

There is always a reason why it can't or won't happen. And there are just as many ways in which your desire can manifest. Where you focus your attention will create your outcome. If you stop and focus on why it won't work, it will never work. Choose a positive attitude and focus on the results you want to receive. Do not waver in your attention to the outcome. When you focus on what you want, you will always get it.

◇ ◇ ◇ ◇

I am dedicated to my goals. I focus on the result I want to achieve, not the reasons why they can't happen. There are infinite possibilities and ways in which my dreams will manifest. I show up daily by taking action. When I align my action with my results, I receive my desires every time.

◇ ◇ ◇ ◇

What reasons can I abandon and replace with results?

I AM IN TOUCH WITH MY WHY.

Why you do what you do is the most important identifier for your success. Whether you want to lose weight, quit an addiction, change jobs or relationships, find a new group of friends, or start your own business, your why matters. Whatever you desire, get clear about your why.

Why you do it will help you focus clearly on your reasons to create the results you desire. When you do things from love, you are aligned with your highest truth and success will be achieved.

◇ ◇ ◇ ◇

I am in touch with why I do what I do. I let my personal focus guide me forward. I am connected to my heart center, which is surrounded by love. I speak clearly and align my action to my intentions. Everything I do is part of my bigger plan, which connects me to my why.

◇ ◇ ◇ ◇

What is my why for doing what I want to do?

EVERYTHING HAS A HONEYMOON STAGE.

It is fun to jump into new relationships, jobs, projects, or places, but be honest with yourself and see that everything always has a honeymoon stage. If you are unhappy with an area of your life and you are planning on making a change, recognize the change will be beneficial. But until you address the core problem, the excitement of the new change will wear off.

If you are unhappy in your career and change jobs, you may be happier temporarily. As the excitement of the new wears off, you will be left with the same internal struggle. It's time to be honest with yourself: until you look at the real problem, the honeymoon phase will just mask the pain.

◇ ◇ ◇ ◇

I am not covering up my pain by fleeing to new opportunities. I address my issues so I can heal and remove them for good. I am not in the honeymoon stage of my life. I embrace the newness but keep the excitement alive by being present and attentive with my needs.

◇ ◇ ◇ ◇

What problem am I trying to escape by jumping
into something new?

THE DOMINO EFFECT OF BEING KIND WILL SHOW UP IN EVERY AREA OF MY LIFE.

Everything you do, and everyone you have met is part of your life story. Everything is always connected. When you are compassionate to others and use kindness as your approach, you will see the results of this in every area of your life.

The biggest struggles you currently face could use a little more compassion and kindness. When you approach problems with an attitude of kindness and love, you will get results faster. Think of your current struggles and send kindness to them.

◇ ◇ ◇ ◇

I am kind. I am love. I focus my attention on being there for others through compassion and love. I know that being kind to others ripples out into every area of my life. When I am nice to others, I feel good about myself. I know we help each other feel more grounded and safer because kindness wins.

◇ ◇ ◇ ◇

How can I be kinder to others?

WHAT I DO TODAY HAS THE POTENTIAL TO IMPROVE ALL OF MY TOMORROWS.

Your actions right now are the most important. Don't worry about yesterday or anything that has happened in your past. From a manifesting standpoint, the only thing that matters is your attention in this moment. Focus on the outcome and achieving what you desire. Pay attention to your thoughts and how they align with your desired outcome. What you do today is important. It will determine your tomorrow.

◇ ◇ ◇ ◇

Starting now, I focus forward. I align my energy with love and support. I will achieve my goal by taking action today. I let go of my past, for today is the only day that matters. It is never too late to start again. Today is my new beginning. What I do today has the potential to improve all my tomorrows.

◇ ◇ ◇ ◇

What can I do today to improve my tomorrow?

I AM AT PEACE WITH WHERE I AM.

It's going to be okay. The majority of your thoughts have been focused on the problem. You have not given yourself a mental break. Forgive yourself and use self-compassion as a tool to move you out of this difficult situation. Healing can occur when you take your focus off the situation. When you accept where you are, you can begin to move forward into where you want to be.

◇ ◇ ◇ ◇

I am at peace. There is nothing to change or shift. Through every experience, I learn more about my true self. I am not wounded or damaged. All is in the right order. Everything I experience is part of my deepest heart's desire. I am growing and learning more about myself, and that is the greatest gift of all. I am at peace with where I am, for it is helping me become who I want to be.

◇ ◇ ◇ ◇

With what do I need to make peace?

I'M OVER THIS LESSON.
I AM DONE.

Life is like a giant classroom. You get to take courses and study different topics: self-worth, humility, financial security, boredom, love, forgiveness, and so on. If you are currently in a situation that feels troublesome, ask what you can learn. You will get your lesson and move through. If you get to a place where you are over it, declare you are done. "I don't want to learn this anymore," and move on. Ask yourself what you want to learn and focus on a new topic. Maybe you are sick of trying so hard to please others. Maybe your efforts have exhausted you. Declare you are over this lesson and move on. Start to put your needs first and you will feel the approval you wanted all along.

◇ ◇ ◇ ◇

I am over this. I am sick of feeling this way and choose not to vibrate at this level anymore. I leave this lesson behind and embrace new opportunities to grow. I am no longer stuck in my fear, and I remove what no longer works in my life. I am over this lesson. I am done.

◇ ◇ ◇ ◇

What lesson am I done with?

NONE OF MY EXPERIENCES DEFINE WHO I AM.

You are the sum of all your experiences, but you are more than what you go through. Don't let your burdens bring you down. The problems you face do not define you. Your focus is not on the situation, but how you perceive the situation.

See each experience as an exploration of self and an opportunity for you to practice more love. Your choices align with your greater plan, but don't get stuck in thinking you are what you do.

◇ ◇ ◇ ◇

I am more than my experiences. I am not what I do. I am bigger than my expressions of life. I believe in my greatness and challenge myself to try new things. When I try new experiences, I grow and become more of who I really want to be.

◇ ◇ ◇ ◇

What experience have I been wrapping my identity in?

I CAN CHANGE DIRECTIONS.

You may be called to look at your life and refocus your direction. Every day is an opportunity to start again. All of your past experiences have led you to where you are today. Remove all regret and frustration associated with feeling as though you aren't where you should be. Now is an ideal time to look at your own past and make changes that will put you on a fresh path. Don't judge your past with criticism but seek to understand what choices helped you gain clarity to move forward today.

◇ ◇ ◇ ◇

I accept my life as an exploration of self and personal discovery. I am always growing and changing, which leads me to deeper understandings of my truth. Every choice I have ever made is part of a big-picture plan. I align with my heart to help me move forward. It is time to change directions and let go of my past. I am open to living my life in new, exciting ways. I take on new directions in my life with joy and confidence.

◇ ◇ ◇ ◇

What new beginning am I being called to?

Day 330

I ALLOW MY IMAGINATION TO EXPLORE OPTIONS FOR DIFFICULT SITUATIONS.

If you are in a difficult situation, consider a more playful approach. You are overthinking the problem, which is preventing you from seeing a result. Instead of focusing on the situation, turn to your imagination and let it lead the way. Your imagination is more powerful than any logic.

◇ ◇ ◇ ◇

My imagination helps me solve problems in my life. Instead of overthinking it or overanalyzing outcomes, I turn to my playful heart and imagine different situations playing out. When I am in touch with my true self, my imagination is active and full of love.

◇ ◇ ◇ ◇

What problem can I solve by tapping into my imagination?

I BELIEVE THINGS ARE SHIFTING IN MY FAVOR.

It doesn't matter where you come from, what your background is, or what happened in the past. You have the capacity to turn things around. Believe things are falling into place and everything is working out in your favor.

Focus on the steps you've taken to help put yourself in a better position. You've made some great choices, and your ship is coming in. Plan out your next steps and focus on the long-term solution. Review your focus with enthusiasm, and you will achieve what you truly desire. Trust that all of the work you've done will produce wonderful results. There is nothing to do, no need to worry. Sometimes it takes a while to see a return on your investments, both energetic and financial. Be patient and know it is on its way to you.

◇ ◇ ◇ ◇

My ship has come in. All of my hard work is now rewarded. This is a time of great celebration, as my efforts have been achieved. I believe in the power of my future, and everything is now turning out for the best. I believe things are always shifting in my favor and the world is on my side.

◇ ◇ ◇ ◇

What evidence that things are working out can I celebrate?

INDECISION DOES NOT LIVE IN MY HEART.

You may be experiencing a pause in action. Now is not the time to rest. Be bold and assert yourself and your true desires. Don't let indecision derail you or prevent you from moving forward. When you are indecisive, it is because you are over-thinking the outcome or worried about what others will think. Instead, drop to your heart to gain the clarity you seek.

◇ ◇ ◇ ◇

I am ambitious with my focus, and I move forward with clarity. I don't overthink situations because I release my fear and act from a place of love. All of my choices are guided by love. I am supported, and my heart will show me the way.

◇ ◇ ◇ ◇

What desire needs more clarity?

"

I Compliment Myself Daily.

"

I COMPLIMENT MYSELF DAILY.

Your inner dialogue is exhausted from all of the self-sabotage and hate. The negative energy you hold about yourself is hurting your heart. You are far more beautiful, kind, intelligent, and loving than you realize. Release all the negativity you have with love and compassionate focus. When you can turn your negative energy into loving light, you will feel more connected to your best self.

Compliment yourself instead of turning to negativity. Go a full day without talking badly about yourself. Each time you fall into negative self-talk, be aware and give yourself a compliment. When you are aware of your thoughts, they create your reality. Turn your negative energy into positive light.

◇ ◇ ◇ ◇

I am aware of my conscious thoughts, and I align with love. I choose positive thoughts, and I talk nicely about myself to myself. I compliment myself by celebrating my uniqueness. I let go of my insecurities and replace them with love.

◇ ◇ ◇ ◇

What area of my life needs the most compliments?

I AM ALWAYS GROWING
AND NEEDING NEW TEACHERS.

Pay attention to the guidance you receive right now. You are living your answered prayer. You may have yearned for new teachers, books, courses, friends, or situations to come into your life. You may notice your past approach and relationships no longer work the way they use to.

You may be on a spiritual path of new self-discovery, looking for deeper understanding of yourself and the world. Your old way of doing things or relating to others no longer feels the same. This is because you are always growing. Instead of holding on to old behaviors and people, allow yourself to spread your wings and fly. You are coming into a new time of great understanding. Allow yourself to be guided and open to new teachers.

◇ ◇ ◇ ◇

I am always changing and growing into who I am supposed to be. I recognize my need for greater awareness, and I seek out mentors, teachers, authors, friends, and situations that align with my highest intention. I release old patterns, people, and ways of being, so I can welcome in the new energy that supports my growth and expansion. I release my old habits and embrace a more loving perspective.

◇ ◇ ◇ ◇

What teacher am I being called to study with?

THINGS GO GRAY WHEN
I FORGET TO PLAY.

You are taking yourself too seriously. The situation you are in may require a less constricted approach, meaning don't look at it as black and white. When you struggle to find meaning in a troubling situation, you are often looking at it from one point of view. Instead of overthinking what happened or what will happen, play and you will watch the situation resolve itself.

When you take your attention off of what bothers you, the experience has time to heal. The world is full of opportunities for you to lighten up and be more light-hearted. Things will naturally fall into place when you play with the world.

◇ ◇ ◇ ◇

I play my way to happiness. I am connected to my joyful self, and I bring more fun into everything I do. The situations that cause me the most stress are healed by my loving attention to the lighthearted nature of life. I don't take myself so seriously, and this lets the situation heal.

◇ ◇ ◇ ◇

How can I bring more fun into a troubling situation?

I PROTECT MY ENERGY.

There are energetic shifts happening on the planet all the time. As things shift, you feel the vibration. Many people feel this vibration and turn to fear and negativity. You can choose to disengage with this low energy and attach yourself to love and light. Possibilities are open to you when you follow the light.

When you protect your energy, you become a source of inspiration for others. You are a light worker on the edge of thought, helping others become their best selves. This is a natural evolution of your own self-development. You grow more into who you really are and allow your true light to shine. Be clear with your focus and align with love and inspiration.

◇ ◇ ◇ ◇

I am in protected by love and light. I turn away all negativity and only allow love into my life. I am inspired and connected to my joy. When I align my intentions with my soul's purpose, I am a light worker for others. I hold the positive intentions and send peace and love out into the world. I am love and inspiration, and I am connected to my truth. I protect my energy by aligning with love.

◇ ◇ ◇ ◇

How can I protect my energy from negative thoughts and people?

I GIVE MYSELF WHAT I NEEDED MOST AS A CHILD.

There is a piece of you that is hurting, stuck in pain, and feeling unloved. This piece of us is often left over from childhood. When we are children, the world revolves around us until something happens and we don't get our way or we see something we don't understand or the world reflects a situation that doesn't bring us joy. We then protect ourselves from feeling hurt. As we grow into adults, there are certain parts of us that still need love, care, and attention, so show up for yourself fully by revisiting your childhood and the situations that need more love. Ask yourself, "What did I need that I never got?" And as an adult, give yourself what you need most.

◇ ◇ ◇ ◇

I show up for myself in loving ways. I am here for me and give myself what I need most in life. I am loved, I am supported, and I am cared for. I forgive those who have hurt me, and I allow myself to be my own best friend. I give myself what I needed most as a child: love, care, and attention.

◇ ◇ ◇ ◇

What did I need as a child but never got enough of?

I DO MY PART.

Pablo Picasso said, "Inspiration exists, but it has to find you working." Making your dreams come true is not a passive process. You have to do the work and show up for your part. Sitting on your meditation pillow, repeating mantras, or visualizing (although good methods) will never produce the outcome—until you take action and do the work.

You must step forward and be in the process of creating in order for the universe to support you. Do your part and show up fully. If you feel stuck and don't know which action to take, declare this out loud. Throw your hands up and say, "I need guidance. What action should I take?" The first inspiration that comes to you is the action for you to move on. Do your part, and the Universe will show up and reward your efforts.

◇ ◇ ◇ ◇

I am showing up for my dreams by taking action daily. I am aligned with the Universe, and we create together. I do my part, and the Universe supports all my actions. I am dedicated to my plan, and I focus forward.

◇ ◇ ◇ ◇

How can I show up fully and take action?

I'VE OUTGROWN WHAT I ONCE NEEDED TO GROW INTO.

Celebrate where you are because you've worked so hard to get right where you are. But where you are going looks nothing like where you have been, and now is the time to let go of what you think you want for your life and let the life that is trying to emerge come into focus. Holding on to things that no longer work keeps us stuck and paralyzed with fear. Release the tension and let yourself grow forward as you move into the next chapter of your life. You have learned the lessons you needed, and what once worked for you is no longer helping you. It is time to let go and move forward with more courageous focus and trust that the Universe has a plan greater than yours. The life that is trying to emerge is your utopia.

◇ ◇ ◇ ◇

My life is a creative adventure, and I am in the driver's seat. I get to choose what I want and don't want to experience by focusing on my intentions. I let go of everything that no longer works, releasing people, places, ideas, and beliefs that do not serve me. As I let go, I invite in new beginnings and trust that the right opportunities will come to me.

◇ ◇ ◇ ◇

What have I outgrown that is ready to be released?

GROWTH SPURTS INDUCE FEAR, BUT THERE IS NOTHING TO BE AFRAID OF.

You may be on a spiritual or self-development path and awakening to a new level of your potential. When this happens, you step into a new area of life, one you have never experienced. This will bring fear to the surface. Insecurities that have not been addressed will show up and scream louder than before. Be kind to yourself and know this is part of the process. Your growth spurt is a beautiful thing. Do not shy away from your greatness by letting your fear stop you. When you address your fear, you can move through it.

◇ ◇ ◇ ◇

I am not limited by my fears. My thoughts are loving and aligned with my truth, and I am in integrity. When I grow and become more of who I really am, my insecurity will reveal fears. This is part of my heroic journey, and there is nothing to be afraid of. The fears are just surface lies trying to keep me playing small. I embrace my truth and ignore the fear, for my dreams are worth it and I am full of unlimited potential.

◇ ◇ ◇ ◇

What fear do I have to address in order to reach my goal?

THEY ARE NOT JUDGING ME.

You spend a generous amount of time worrying about what others think of you. When you are in public, you assume others are thinking about you and judging you. This thought process keeps you from being true to yourself.

You are so worried about what they think of you that you are taking attention off of yourself and your ability to reach your own potential. When you see others who give you a discerning eye or a disapproving glance, recognize they are reflecting your own insecurities.

If you feel unlovable, you may hear rude comments. It isn't the comments that made you feel unlovable. This was already your experience of self. To feel more confident in social situations, focus on self-love and approval.

◇ ◇ ◇ ◇

Other people do not control me. When others say something that hurts my feelings, I know it is not about me. I can't control what others say to me, but I can control my reaction to what they say. I choose self-love, and I approve of myself. There is only one of me in all eternity. I am uniquely me. I am nonjudgmental and judgment-free.

◇ ◇ ◇ ◇

What steps will I take to release judgment?

I CAN'T CHANGE WHAT I DON'T ADDRESS.

Get honest with yourself about everyone and every situation in your life. What is not working? It is time to stop making excuses and address situations and relationships? Be accountable for your life and relationships. Do not compromise. Self-destructive behaviors will become worse if you don't acknowledge them. Be honest with where you are right now so you can address what needs fixing.

◇ ◇ ◇ ◇

I am accountable for all of my experiences. I am honest with myself about what is not working, and I release it with love. I take full responsibility for my direction in life by reassessing where I am. If there is anything that doesn't work for me, I let it go. I trust the situation will be replaced with love and positive energy.

◇ ◇ ◇ ◇

What do I need to address that I have been avoiding?

THERE IS NO REALITY, ONLY PERCEPTION.

You have a view of life that is personal to you and filtered through your beliefs, actions, and experiences. Acknowledge your past, but don't be controlled by it. To live a happy life, recognize your filters, and be compassionate so that they don't distort your perceptions or mislead your decision-making. You might be viewing the world through a filter of past events, which controls your present and dictates your future. Take care not to let fears from the past replay in your mind. If you don't acknowledge that you have fears or limiting beliefs from the past that could be controlling your behavior, you will feel powerless. Let your perceptions be fresh and new and grounded in facts of the current situation, not the past ones.

◇ ◇ ◇ ◇

I am not a victim of my past. I understand my past is in my past. I focus on my present and make choices from a loving place. I am aligned with my heart's desires, and I let love lead the way. I do not judge myself for my beliefs or past experiences. Instead, I look closely at my filters of the world and remove limiting beliefs and thought limitations.

◇ ◇ ◇ ◇

What filter has distorted my reality?

I TEACH PEOPLE HOW TO TREAT ME.

Look at all of your relationships and see what they have in common: you. How do people in those relationships treat you? You either show people to treat you with love and respect or you don't. You are, on some level, responsible for any mistreatment in your life. You have, on some level, allowed it to persist.

Instead of blaming or complaining about your relationships, own your true self-worth and stand up for yourself with dignity and pride. You can refocus any relationship. Even patterns that have persisted for fifteen years can be addressed by negotiating your real worth. Commit to yourself from a place of love and light, not fear and doubt. Let your relationships be full of love.

◇ ◇ ◇ ◇

I commit to raising the vibration of all of my relationships. I teach people how to treat me because I show them my worth. I don't stand for harm. I only have supportive, caring relationships. I am connected to light and full of love. I love myself, and this extends out into all my relationships.

◇ ◇ ◇ ◇

How have I taught other people to treat me?

SITUATIONS DON'T HURT. EXPECTATIONS DO.

Expectations can be both wonderful and damaging. Sometimes when we build up how we would like an outcome to unfold, the reality of what happens is a letdown. Take a moment to reflect on what you wanted to happen. If there are situations causing you pain, look at what your expectations were. Did you want something to happen that didn't? Or maybe things didn't work out according to your plan. Expectations hurt your ability to enjoy life and accept the process.

When you set a goal or begin a new relationship, release the expectation and focus on the feeling instead of the outcome. How does it feel to put your goal into action? This is the energy you want to hold. Leave the how and when to the Universe. You will always get exactly what you need when you need it.

◇ ◇ ◇ ◇

I release all expectations and allow myself to be in the flow of life. I embrace the journey and let things unfold naturally. I am in no hurry, and there is no rush to get where I want to go. The situations I am in are part of my life plan. I accept them as though I had chosen them myself. I release all expectations and trust things are as they should be.

◇ ◇ ◇ ◇

What expectations did I have of the situation that is causing me the most pain?

Day 346

THERE IS PLENTY OF TIME.

You may feel frustrated because what you want has not yet arrived. When you are manifesting and working toward your dreams, instant gratification is what you seek. But patience is about being at peace with the process. Recognize there is a divine timing to your desire, and it will come to you at the perfect time.

When you are impatient, it energetically holds the process. Because you focus on what you want not being here, you actually put more attention on the lack. Breathe in deeply and ask yourself what you still need to learn. You will receive guidance to help you around the situation.

◇ ◇ ◇ ◇

There is plenty of time, and I am in no hurry. My dreams will manifest at the perfect time and in the right order. I release all expectations around my life and goals and know I am being divinely led. There is always plenty of time.

◇ ◇ ◇ ◇

What am I rushing?

Day 347

I CHOOSE TO BE SEEN IN MY RADIANT TOTALITY, AND I FEEL SAFE AND SUPPORTED DOING SO.

You have a gorgeous, radiant light within you that shines so bright. It is time for you to honor and see your own greatness. You may be spending extra time focusing on how you feel unworthy or not quite ready to step forward into your ideal life, but today's mantra is an affirmation to your true self. Honor yourself by being the light and know that you are supported and loved. When you are true to yourself and follow through on your own heart's desires, you will see more support and love from the Universe, as well as, those around you. If you don't feel supported, it could be because you don't believe in yourself. Instead of focusing on the lack, see yourself as the radiant, loving being you are.

◇ ◇ ◇ ◇

Everything I am is love and light. I refuse to be held back by my insecurities and frustrations. I am ready to step forward fully into my greatness—it is time for me to shine. Everything I have ever done has prepared me for this moment. I am ready.

◇ ◇ ◇ ◇

In which situation can I visualize myself being
seen and appreciated?

SOME THINGS FALL APART, SO THEY CAN COME BACK TOGETHER AT A BETTER TIME.

There is a time for everything in your life, and sometimes things need to fall apart so they can come back together in the future at a better time. Do not worry about the transition or letting go, as the release is essential for your happiness. Let go of worry and fear and trust that everything in your life happens to help support your greatest good. Holding on to what no longer works is keeping you stuck. Turn all your attention to what it is you really want, which is to feel good, supported, and loved. Let things go that are meant to be let go of and trust divine timing will bring it back into your life if it is in your highest good.

◇ ◇ ◇ ◇

I let go of what is meant to be released. The first thing that comes to mind is the thing I need to let go of. It is okay to feel a loss, for the amount of love I had for it is real, but I trust the timing of everything in my life. I do not manipulate or hold on to things that are meant to be released. I trust that, in time, if we are supposed to come back together again, we will, but until then, I let go with grace and ease.

◇ ◇ ◇ ◇

What am I holding on to that is ready to be released?

Day 349

I ALIGN MY THOUGHTS WITH LOVE.

Moment-to-moment thinking is where your power lies. When you talk down to yourself, you hurt your capacity to let love in. But each moment, you can cultivate an awareness of expansion by catching your negative voice in action. When you hear your inner dialog turn to negativity, surround it with love and repeat kind words: "You are doing the best you can, and it is all going to be okay." You will get clear results with consistency.

The more you can stop negativity and fear-based thoughts, the happier you will be. It doesn't matter what yesterday held or what your thoughts were while you were growing up. The only place you ever have any power is right here, right now. Align your thoughts with love.

◇ ◇ ◇ ◇

The place I can make the most change in my life is right here, right now, with my thoughts. I align my energy to love and release all negative, fear-based thoughts. I speak kindly to myself and uplift others with love.

◇ ◇ ◇ ◇

What is a loving thought about myself?

EVERYTHING IS RELATIVE.

Every day, you are changing and growing. The person you were when you stepped into the situation currently causing your frustration is not the same person you are today. The situation has helped you learn more about what is important to you. It is necessary to reevaluate and see if your current situation is serving you.

Everything is relative and part of your life plan. When you can look objectively at situations, you will see the path to take. Be willing to let go of situations that once caused you pleasure but now cause pain.

◇ ◇ ◇ ◇

I understand everything is relative and part of a bigger life plan. The Universe supports me. My decision to move forward is based on love. I learn from all of my situations and see the power in letting go.

◇ ◇ ◇ ◇

What situations have I outgrown?

I FOUND MY HAPPY.

You may be trying to get happy, but the happiness that you desire is already within you. Instead of making your happiness contingent on external forces or a future event yet to manifest, choose to be happy in this moment. Focus all of your energy into gratitude and fill your heart with love.

All of the work you do, the books you read, the courses you take, and self-development tools you use are part of your divine life plan. Release the need to get there and have the instant hit of "having it all figured out." Self-improvement comes from a compassionate approach and one that can be a joyful journey. Enjoy the teachers you resonate with and let your happy shine through. You already have what you seek. Just let it be and trust you have arrived.

◇ ◇ ◇ ◇

I open my heart to happiness and joy. I embrace all of the good in my life, and I am thankful for what is. I feel loved, and I am supported. All of my dreams are coming true, and I choose happiness right now.

◇ ◇ ◇ ◇

What is working great in my life?

INSTEAD OF TRYING TO GET ATTENTION, I GIVE IT.

You may be trying to get the attention of another person but feel like they are not seeing you for who you are. Your attitude may be desperate or needy. Instead of trying to get attention, try to give it. By giving what you seek, you will, in return, get what you want. Giving attention to others is part of your soul's purpose, and when you serve, you get out of your own way.

◇ ◇ ◇ ◇

Beautiful things do not need attention. They are as they are. I am a beautiful person who does good deeds. I do not need attention for my acts of kindness. I seek out ways in which I can be of service and help others. Instead of trying to get attention, I give it to others.

◇ ◇ ◇ ◇

How can I be of service?

I'M NOT AFRAID TO INVEST
IN MY DREAMS.

Putting energy, time, and financial resources into something you believe in will never lead you astray. When your heart and head are aligned and you're focused on your desire, you give it all you got. Investing in your dreams is investing in yourself. When you show up for your dreams, you are saying you matter.

A farmer does not yell at his crop to grow faster. He knows there is a season of growing and a season of harvest. If you are investing in your dream, give yourself time to see the harvest. Don't abandon your dream because it isn't growing fast enough. Great things take time to develop, but when you water them with love, you will be rewarded in more ways than you can ever imagine. Don't give up on yourself or your dreams.

◇ ◇ ◇ ◇

I spend time, money, and energy on the things that are important to me. I am not afraid to invest in my dreams because I know I will see the return. I believe in my heart I am doing the right thing for me, so I move forward with confidence, faith, and a knowing that all of my actions will be rewarded. The Universe supports my dream by watering it with love. I will see the rewards soon, and all of my hard work will be worth it.

◇ ◇ ◇ ◇

What dream will I invest in?

Day 354

I AM SELECTIVE WITH MY CHOICES.

Becoming more selective with your activities, friends, social engagements, and habits will serve you right now. When you are selective with how you spend your time, you place specialness on what you value. If you are overextending yourself or giving away too much of your time, your energy will be depleted.

Having a close group of sincere friends versus a wide range of people you kind of know will help you feel more connected and grounded. Make more choices with a selective process. Choosing how you spend your time and with whom cultivates self-respect.

◇ ◇ ◇ ◇

I love myself enough to do what I want when I want. I don't waste time on people, places, or things that waste my energy. I focus on loving thoughts and spend my time with people I love. Together we accomplish great things because we support one another with compassion, hope, and joy.

◇ ◇ ◇ ◇

What choice can I be more selective with?

PROCRASTINATION IS A DEAD DESIRE.

Procrastination happens when you are not in touch with your heart's desires. Any activity worthy of your effort should be approached with love and tackled with gusto. You don't have to do it all in one day, but taking it in bits and pieces can help.

When you procrastinate, you show yourself that your activities do not matter, which sends a message to yourself that you are unworthy of your desires. If you put off projects, find a way to tap into the reason you love them. This will help you feel connected to the projects and help you move forward with more clarity.

◇ ◇ ◇ ◇

I do not waste time on frivolous things. I am focused on my plan, and I do not procrastinate. When things need to be done, I do them with care. I take one step at a time to reach my goals. I focus on mini goals within the big goal to help me conquer my fears. I am in touch with my desires, which leads me forward.

◇ ◇ ◇ ◇

What have I been procrastinating?

Day 356

I EXPRESS HUMILITY.

When you shift directions, change carriers, relationships, move, or try something new, you will be stepping out of your comfort zone. Letting go of how others perceive you will serve you well through all changes. Maybe you were fired from your job and you took a position at a new company that pays a lot less. Express humility.

Perhaps you went through a tough divorce, and the other person has remarried, but you are still single. Express humility. Being humble through your life changes will help you surrender to what is. You can release expectations about how your life should look or how it was supposed to turn out by returning to your heart center, which is humble and full of humility.

◇ ◇ ◇ ◇

I express divine grace through my detachment to self. I am not my situations or my problems. I am separate from my life drama. I express kindness and love to all by accepting myself as I am today. I am humble and honest with who I am and where I stand. I express humility.

◇ ◇ ◇ ◇

How can I be more humble?

Day 357

I DON'T HANG ON TO MOMENTS.

Hanging onto moments once they have gone will keep you from moving forward. There are joyful lessons to be learned in your current experience, but hanging onto the past keeps you from receiving these rewards. Life goes on and will unfold ever expansively. But when you spend your time thinking about the past, you hurt your present and future.

Be honest with yourself and see if you are hanging onto something in your past. It could be a relationship, a job, the money you earn, or a place you lived. Whatever the situation, if you are stuck in a moment, you will invite more shame into your life. When you bring your attention to the now, you invite others into your life. Let go of past moments, so you can be present in this moment.

◇ ◇ ◇ ◇

I am present in my life and free of past burdens. I don't hang on to memories or replay them in the present. I am focused on my current reality and free of fear. I am happy and focused on this moment, for right now is all I have.

◇ ◇ ◇ ◇

What moment do I keep replaying in my mind?

Day 358

I ENJOY THE BEAUTY OF BECOMING.

We are always in the process of becoming. What you want is on its way to you, but you must be present to lessons and the learning available to you along the way. The in-between, the space that is not here or there, is where real growth and transformation happens. Stay focused on what you want and appreciate who you are becoming. Enjoy the beautiful journey of becoming.

◇ ◇ ◇ ◇

I am okay with where I am because there is great learning here. I am becoming more of who I want to be, and the lessons I learn along the way are just as important as the outcome. The art of becoming is becoming on me as I dive deep into the moment and allow myself to be in a transition, for all of my life is ever-changing, and I allow myself to grow.

◇ ◇ ◇ ◇

In what ways can I appreciate my current circumstances more?

THERE ARE NO ACCIDENTS.

You are on the right path as long as you stay focused on your heart's desire. You may feel like you have gotten off track, but there are no mistakes. Everything you are currently experiencing is part of your ultimate life plan.

Realize your negative thoughts and their associated emotions result from your mind. No matter what terrible choices you've made, or what horrible event has happened, you have the choice to see it as a blessing or a curse. The Universe is always leading you to path of greater understanding and reward. See the opportunities in all situations and you will be free of worry.

◇ ◇ ◇ ◇

I see everything as an opportunity for growth and awareness. I am living my life as an example of what's possible, and I live it on purpose. There are no accidents or wrong turns. Every step I take is part of a perfect plan devised by my higher self. The Universe supports me and guides me to freedom.

◇ ◇ ◇ ◇

What mistake can I forgive myself for?

Day 360

THIS IS NOT MY PRACTICE LIFE.

No more excuses. It's time to get it done. This is not a practice life. Right now this is all you have. Give your life the meaning you crave. It is your mission to give it all you've got. When you blame, worry, or make excuses about why it can't be done, someone else with less is doing more. Give yourself permission to be all you really are meant to be and you will amaze yourself. A desire deep in your heart is ready to come out. Show the world what you are made of by being true to your heart's desires.

◇ ◇ ◇ ◇

I am capable of everything I put my mind to. I achieve greatness by giving it my all. This is not my practice life. This is the real deal. I show up with gusto and align with my heart's purpose. I am love and a reflection of light. I share all that is good.

◇ ◇ ◇ ◇

What do I need to give myself more credit for?

THE LESS I KNOW ABOUT "HOW," THE BETTER.

Having a can-do attitude and a go-get-'em spirit will give you the results you desire. Go for it and make it happen. When you have a new project or goal you are working on, you may hesitate because you don't know what path to take. The path that has been paved before might not work best for you. Just because it has worked for others doesn't mean it's your path. Don't be afraid to go your own way and carve out a new plan. The world's greatest innovators, inspirational teachers, and thought leaders do things their own way. Instead of looking to see what has been done or what is possible, believe in your heart that you can do it and go for it with your imagination and knowledge.

◇ ◇ ◇ ◇

I am not afraid of my own greatness. I shine my light bright and do what works for me. I refuse to accept others' opinions and views about my life and direction. I do what is right for me and what feels good for me. No one can stand in my way when I align with my truth. My plan is unique to me. I fearlessly move forward.

◇ ◇ ◇ ◇

What do I want to do that hasn't been done?

I REFUSE TO STAND IN MY OWN WAY.
I BELIEVE IN ALL I CAN BE.

You are more powerful, focused, and capable than you realize. Now more than ever, you are in a position to reach your potential. Pay attention to your senses as they come to life and guide you forward. Your intuition is talking to you. Listen to its message. You are being guided into the next right step, but you must know you are capable.

Everything you have ever done has prepared for this moment. You're ready. Believe in yourself and you will see the manifestation of your heart's truest desire. Hold that faith and let it guide you forward. Only you can allow others to take away your hopes and dreams. Don't get derailed by others. Focus your intentions with love and surround yourself with light.

◇ ◇ ◇ ◇

Everything is connected and part of my divine plan. I am more aware and connected than I have ever been, and this moment is what matters. I refuse to stand in my own way. I believe in everything I can be, and I live my truth daily.

◇ ◇ ◇ ◇

How have I been standing in my own way?

"

I Refuse to Stand In My Own Way. I Believe in All I Can Be.

"

MY FUTURE STARTS TODAY.

Everything you have ever wanted to be is possible. You can start fresh and refocus any time. Today is the most important day of your life, for it determines the rest of your journey. What you do today is the path to your tomorrow.

When you are present in this moment, you have all the power, focus, skills, and energy you need. Release the burdens of your past and focus fully on today. Your future is unwritten, but it can turn out better than you ever imagined with your action today.

◇ ◇ ◇ ◇

I am aligned with love. Love guides every action I take to help me become who I see myself becoming. Tomorrow is unwritten, but I can control my outcome by the actions I take today. I take loving action and direct myself into happiness with light.

◇ ◇ ◇ ◇

What action can I take to create my ideal future?

WHATEVER WILL BE, WILL BE.

The future is not yours to see. What is unfolding is part of a divine plan that will work in your favor. There is no need for you to see the whole picture. Trust the process and be in the journey. When you worry about the future and try to control the outcome, you stop yourself from living your life fully.

Whatever will be, will be. It is part of your truth. Trust you will get what you need when you need it but not a moment sooner. Everything in your life will always work out. Be in the journey of your life and focus forward with compassion and joy.

◇ ◇ ◇ ◇

I have goals I work toward, but I don't hold on or try to manipulate the outcome. I cocreate with the Universe and trust I will get what I need when I need it. The future is not for me to see, but I am comfortable in the unknown. I focus forward, living from my heart. All is in the right order, and everything will work out in my favor. It always does.

◇ ◇ ◇ ◇

How can I be more present in this moment?

THE UNKNOWN IS WHERE I CAN DANCE FULLY WITH LIFE.

The unknown is not something to be feared. The unknown is a space where you can truly come alive. Instead of worrying about the future, let yourself bask in the beauty of potential. The potential is in the moment and the unfolding of your life. Look at life as a dance and embrace the changing situations. With each change comes new opportunity for you to grow and become more of who you are meant to be. Play with each new situation as you push yourself joyfully into the rhythm and flow of life. You will see things with fresh light and more joy.

◇ ◇ ◇ ◇

My life is a dance, and I choose to see things with more grace and ease. As I embrace new situations, I no longer fear the future. The unknown is not something for me to be scared of, but instead I embrace it. I come alive in the space between where I want to be and where I once was. I am fully present in my life and actively create the reality I want.

◇ ◇ ◇ ◇

What current situation can I be more present to?

Find Your Happy Daily Mantras Resources

Shannon here! I'm committed to doing all I can to help you heal, grow, and transform, which is why I've created extra resources to help you feel more connected to your authentic self. This book is one tool, among many, to guide you to make joy and fulfillment your natural way of life. In addition to this book, these resources will support your path to inner peace and connect to the loving light within.

FREE "I AM PEACE" AUDIO MEDITATION

I created a powerful audio meditation that you can download for free to help you align daily with your best self. This meditation is designed to help you overcome anxiety, fear, and self-sabotaging emotions; it will help you maximize your potential and balance your energy. Download the free I AM PEACE audio meditation here: www.playwiththeworld.com/dailymantras/freemediation

FIND YOUR HAPPY DAILY MANTRA DECK

Sometimes you need even more daily motivation, which is why I created an inspirational 56-card mantra deck to go along with this book that will help you align with your best self and play with the world at the same time. My *Find Your Happy Daily Mantra Deck* will help you tune in to the flow of the universe, show yourself compassion when times get tough, and break free from emotional restraints. This dynamic card deck is paired with a guidebook that will help you meditate on the truths contained within each card and live each day with intention.

JOIN THE COMMUNITY

There is a tight-knit, collaborative community on my Shannon Kaiser Facebook and Instagram. Connect with likeminded friends @ShannonKaiserWrites. This is a safe community where I post tools, resources, and daily mantras and inspiration. Share your reflections, your questions, and your brilliant aha moments.

SHARE THE LOVE
#FINDYOURHAPPYDAILYMANTRAS

When you are inspired by messages and mantras in this book, share them on social media using #FindYourHappy or #FindYourHappyDailyMantras. I invite you to take photos of the book cover or any text that inspires you and post to your social media pages, as I am always reposting readers' photos. Just make sure to use the hashtags or tag @ShannonKaiserWrites so I can find you.

FIND YOUR HAPPY AUDIO MEDITATION ALBUM

If you enjoy audio guidance and meditations, you will love the Find Your Happy meditation album. Each track will take you deeper into a meditative state to help support your journey to wholeness. I use these powerful, uplifting meditations in my in-person events and coaching practice. You can access the meditations here:

http://playwiththeworld.com/meditation-albums/